fabulous
frames

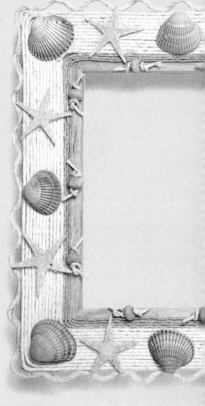

fabulous
frames

DEBORAH
SCHNEEBELI-MORRELL

RD
PRESS

A QUARTO BOOK

First published in Australia in 1995 by RD Press,
a registered business name of
Reader's Digest (Australia) Pty Limited
26–32 Waterloo Street, Surry Hills, NSW 2010

The National Library of Australia Cataloguing-in-Publication Data

Schneebeli-Morrell, Deborah.
Fabulous frames : 35 step-by-step projects for
decorating your own frames.

ISBN 0 86438 795 4.

1. Picture frames and framing. I. Title.

749.7

This book was designed and produced by
Quarto Publishing plc
6 Blundell Street
London N7 9BH

Senior Art Editor Penny Cobb
Designer Karin Skänberg
Senior Editor Kate Kirby
Text Editor Cathy Meeus
Photography Paul Forrester, Laura Wickenden
Illustrator Rob Shone
Prop Research Penny Dawes
Editorial Director Sophie Collins
Art Director Moira Clinch

Typeset in Great Britain by
Central Southern Typesetters, Eastbourne
Manufactured by Eray Scan Pte Ltd,
Singapore
Printed by Star Standard Industries
(Pte) Ltd, Singapore

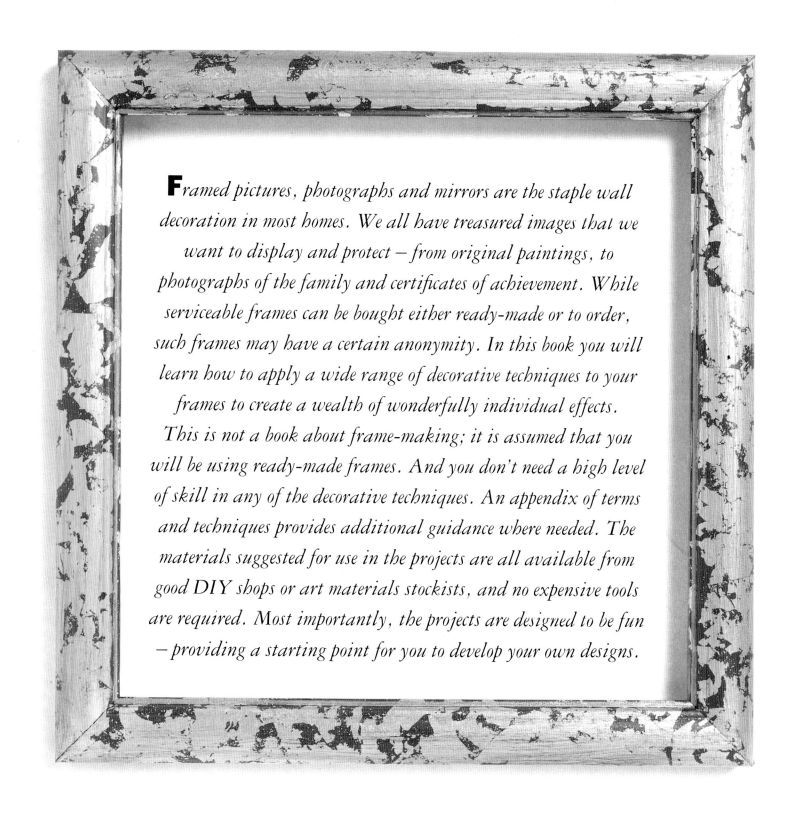

Framed pictures, photographs and mirrors are the staple wall decoration in most homes. We all have treasured images that we want to display and protect – from original paintings, to photographs of the family and certificates of achievement. While serviceable frames can be bought either ready-made or to order, such frames may have a certain anonymity. In this book you will learn how to apply a wide range of decorative techniques to your frames to create a wealth of wonderfully individual effects.

This is not a book about frame-making; it is assumed that you will be using ready-made frames. And you don't need a high level of skill in any of the decorative techniques. An appendix of terms and techniques provides additional guidance where needed. The materials suggested for use in the projects are all available from good DIY shops or art materials stockists, and no expensive tools are required. Most importantly, the projects are designed to be fun – providing a starting point for you to develop your own designs.

Contents

1
Marvellous metal

2
Pretty paper

3
Fortunate finds

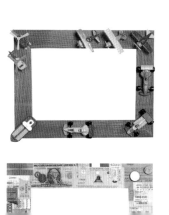

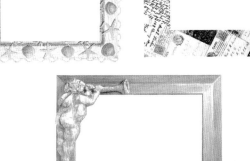

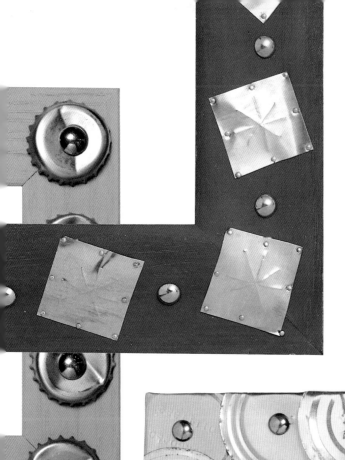

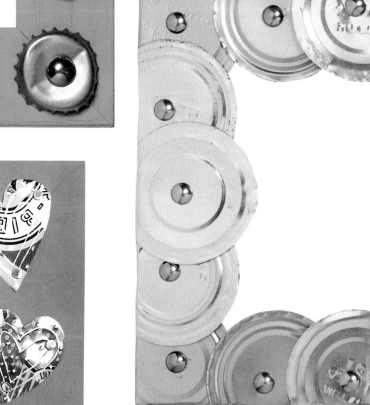

Marvellous metal

Create an original range of frames by applying painted or plain metal shapes to your frame surround. The metal can come from a wide variety of everyday items – cans, bottle tops, and wire, for example – and can be easily cut to make the appliqué shapes you want. Use bright matt colours for the frame bases to provide an effective contrast with the shine of the metal.

Bottle tops

***A** great example of how everyday items can be used to create original decorative effects, this simple frame could be used for a bold, naive image such as a child's painting.*

1 Paint the frame with two coats of green acrylic paint. Allow to dry.

2 Assemble sufficient bottle caps to decorate the frame when positioned equidistantly around the frame. It is a good idea to rub down the tops with fine glasspaper to obtain a consistent appearance. The "fold" in the top that forms when you lever it off from the bottle adds to the overall effect.

3 Make a hole in the centre of each top with a bradawl. Secure the bottle tops in their final positions by hammering a brass upholstery pin through the centre hole.

You will need

- **Small frame with simple rectangular moulding, with a front border approximately 40mm (1½ inches) wide**
- **Approximately 14 bottle caps of the same type**
- **Approximately 14 round-headed brass upholstery nails**

- **Green acrylic paint**
- **Fine glasspaper**
- **Bradawl**
- **Hammer**
- **25 mm (1 inch) flat paint brush**

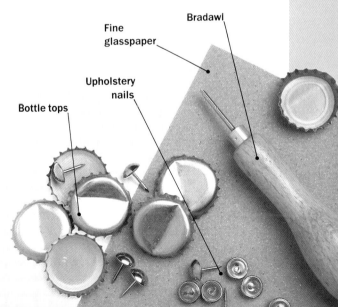

Fine glasspaper

Bradawl

Upholstery nails

Bottle tops

Tin can lids frame

You will need

- Small frame with simple rectangular moulding, with a front border approximately 40mm (1½ inches) wide
- Approximately 20 tin can lids of varying sizes
- Approximately 20 round-headed brass upholstery nails
- Coarse emery paper or glasspaper
- Brass escutcheon pins
- Hammer

This inspirational recycling idea creates a bold frame that could be used for displaying a mirror, three-dimensional objects, or strong, simple images.

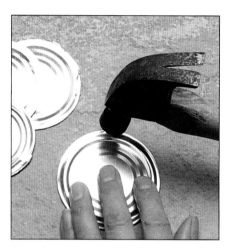

1 The jagged-edged lids are a feature of this frame. An alternative is to use a tin opener which removes lids cleanly, in which case you can skip step 2.

2 Lightly beat the edges of the lids with a hammer on a hard surface to flatten any dangerous jagged edges. To be sure of removing all sharpness, sand the edges with coarse emery paper or coarse glasspaper.

Tin can lids – various

Can opener

Escutcheon pins

Coarse emery paper

Upholstery nails, used in preference to ordinary nails because they have a decorative smooth rounded end.

Hammer

3 Arrange the lids around the frame so that a large lid is positioned in the centre of each side. Alternate the varying colours of metal to achieve a pleasing effect.

4 Position a lid in each corner so that it overlaps the inner and outer edges of the frame. Secure by hammering an upholstery nail through the centre of the lid.

5 Working from each corner towards the centre on each side of the frame in turn, overlap the next lid and secure in the same way. Finally secure the large central lid on each side.

You don't have to use round lids for the frame — any shape lid will do.

Upholstery nails

Escutcheon pins are fine and don't split wood when hammered in.

6 Bend the edges of the lids around the outside of the frame by gently hammering them through a wad of cloth to prevent damage to the appearance of the lids. Make sure that the edges lie flat to the outer edge of the frame.

7 Secure the outside edge of each lid to the frame with two escutcheon pins.

Finished frame
Avoiding the sharp edges, give the finished frame a final polish.

A tin opener that removes lids cleanly does away with jagged edges.

Brass squares frame

The bold impact of the combination of a strong blue background and gold-coloured motifs is exploited in this frame. Follow this design idea or create your own design, perhaps of stars and moons, for a truly contemporary look.

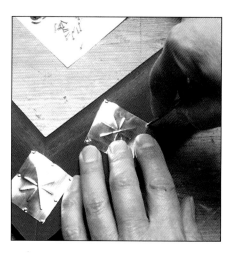

1 Apply two coats of paint to the frame front and edges. Cut twelve 40 mm (1½ inch) squares from the brass sheet using scissors. Smooth any sharp edges with glasspaper. Place the squares on an old magazine or thick wad of newspaper and score a star design in the centre of each with an old ballpoint pen.

2 When the paint is dry, arrange the squares around the frame symmetrically. Vary the orientation of the squares to avoid monotony. With a bradawl, make eight small holes in each of the squares (one in each corner and one in the centre of each side) and continue the holes into the frame. Secure each square in place with eight brass escutcheon pins.

3 Hammer a round-headed brass upholstery nail into the frame between each of the squares.

Hammer

Brass sheet

Escutcheon pins

Bradawl

You will need

- Square frame with curved reverse moulding, with a front border approximately 65 mm (2½ inches) wide
- Thin brass sheet 160 × 120 mm (6¼ × 4½ inches)

- 12 round-headed brass upholstery nails
- Ultramarine acrylic paint
- Old magazine or thick wad of newspaper
- Glasspaper

- Old ballpoint pen
- Brass escutcheon pins
- Scissors
- Small hammer
- Bradawl
- 12 mm (½ inch) flat paint brush

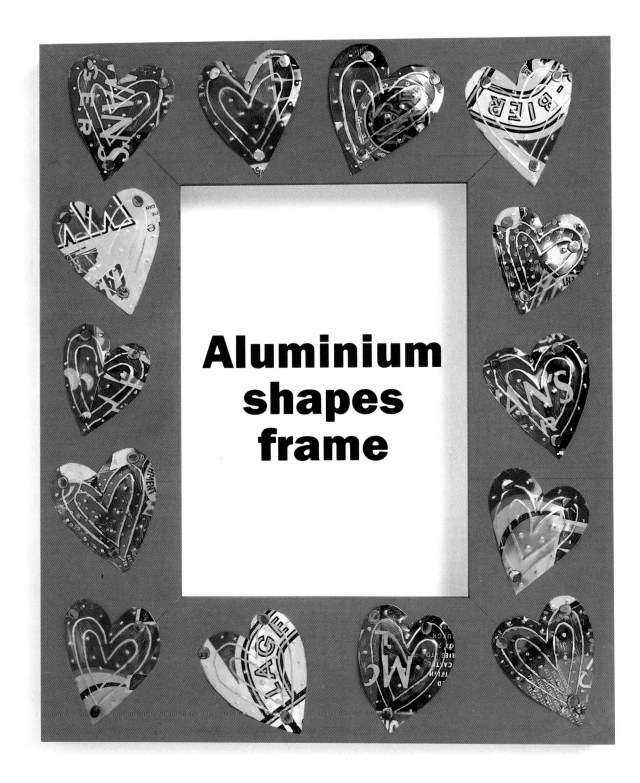

Aluminium shapes frame

This cheerful frame, with its cut-out aluminium hearts and vibrant Mediterranean colours, could be used for a romantic snap taken on holiday. Vary the effect using the same technique with different aluminium shapes and frame colours.

1 Apply two coats of orange paint to the front surface of the frame with the large brush. Allow time for the paint to dry between coats.

2 Apply two coats of magenta to the inner and outside edges of the frame with the small brush, allowing to dry between coats as before.

3 Make initial holes in the cans with a large craft knife, and then use scissors to cut off the tops and bottoms. Trim off any jagged or rough edges.

You will need

- Frame with simple rectangular moulding, with a front border approximately 65 mm (2½ inches) wide
- Five aluminium cans with different printed colours and designs
- 10 mm (⅜ inch) steel tacks
- Large craft knife
- Old magazine or thick wad of newspaper

- Orange and magenta acrylic paint
- Fine glasspaper
- Old ballpoint pen
- Strong scissors
- Small hammer
- Bradawl
- 25 mm (1 inch) and 6mm (¼ inch) flat paint brushes

Steel tacks

Awl for making indentations in the aluminium

Hammer

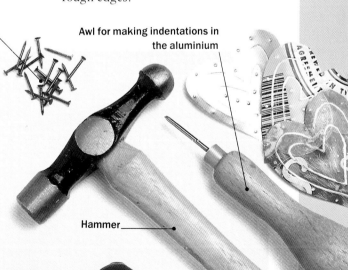

Tubes of acrylic paint — acrylics give a nice solid matt colour.

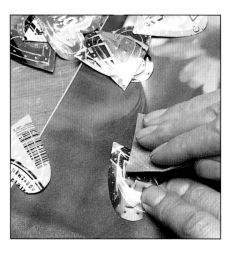

4 Cut heart shapes from the flattened cans, selecting the parts that provide the most interesting colours and patterns. Although the hearts do not need to be identical, none should be too large to fit comfortably within the frame border – about 50 mm (2 inches) from top to bottom is about right. You will need about 14 hearts.

5 Working with the plain side of the hearts uppermost and resting on a magazine or thick wad of newspaper, score a design of concentric heart shapes into the metal using an old ballpoint pen. You will need to press quite hard. Finish the design by adding dots in the middle and around the edge.

6 Using glasspaper, lightly sand the heart shapes on the patterned/coloured side to reveal the scored design picked out in bare metal.

Old ball-point pen for scoring designs.

Geometric shapes – hearts, flowers, stars – the simpler the shape, the easier it is to cut out.

Collect brightly coloured cans.

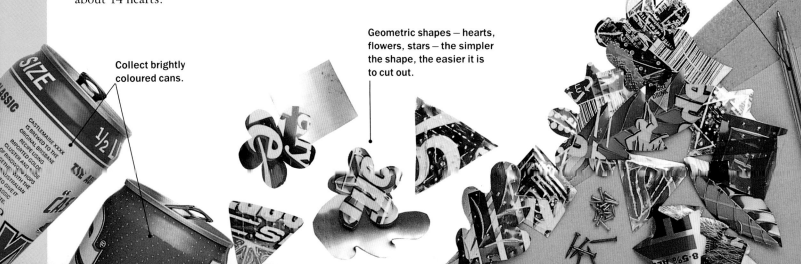

7 Arrange the hearts equidistantly around the frame, placing one in each corner and an equal number along opposing sides. Alternate the angle at which the hearts are positioned to create a lively effect.

8 After making an initial hole through each heart into the frame, secure each heart in position with three steel tacks.

Sandpaper for bringing out the relief design.

Finished frame
When all the hearts are in place, hammer the tacks flush to the frame.

Engraved aluminium frame

You will need

- Rectangular frame with flat moulding
- Thin aluminium sheet larger than the frame
- Metal ruler
- Old (dry) ball-point pen
- Strong scissors
- Small panel pins
- Pencil
- Thick wad of newspaper
- Hammer
- Bradawl

This is a wonderful technique for giving a new lease of life to an old or battered frame as the metal sheeting covers all the wood. You can give full vent to your creativity with engraved designs as complex or as simple as you like.

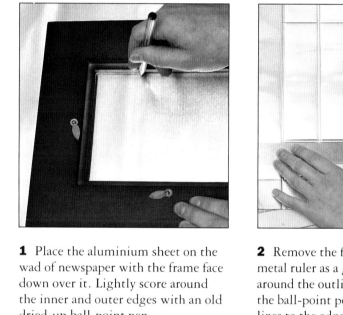

1 Place the aluminium sheet on the wad of newspaper with the frame face down over it. Lightly score around the inner and outer edges with an old dried-up ball-point pen.

2 Remove the frame and using a metal ruler as a guide, score firmly around the outline of the frame with the ball-point pen, extending the lines to the edge of the metal. Add a second scored line inside each of the original lines.

Frame with flat moulding

Aluminium sheet

Hammer

Bradawl for piercing holes

Strong scissors

Panel pins

Wad of newspaper to protect the surface on which you are scoring the aluminium sheet.

Ruler

Ball-point pen

Pencil

3 Score diagonal lines from each inside corner across the centre of the frame. Score an inner border slightly wider than the depth of the frame. Use strong scissors to cut out the centre within the inner border.

4 Snip into the inner corners along the diagonals.

5 Cut off the outer corners of the metal outside the frame area.

Copper and brass sheets. Keep engraved images simple, avoiding too much detail.

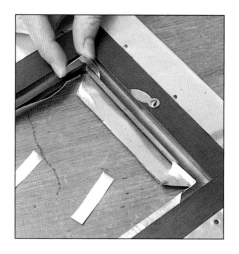

6 Lightly sketch the design of your choice in pencil on the back of the frame. Score the design with the old ball-point pen when you are happy with the effect.

7 When the design is complete, place the frame face down over the aluminium. Position the frame so that it lines up with the scored outline. Bend the outer edges of the aluminium around the back of the frame and smooth it down so that it fits snugly around the edges. Secure with small panel pins, spaced about 25 mm (1 inch) apart.

8 Bend back the inner edges. Insert a small L-shaped strip of aluminium into each of the inner corners to provide a neat finish. Bend the aluminium over the rebate and smooth down.

Finished frame A soft cloth was used to remove the finger marks and to bring out the lustre of the metal.

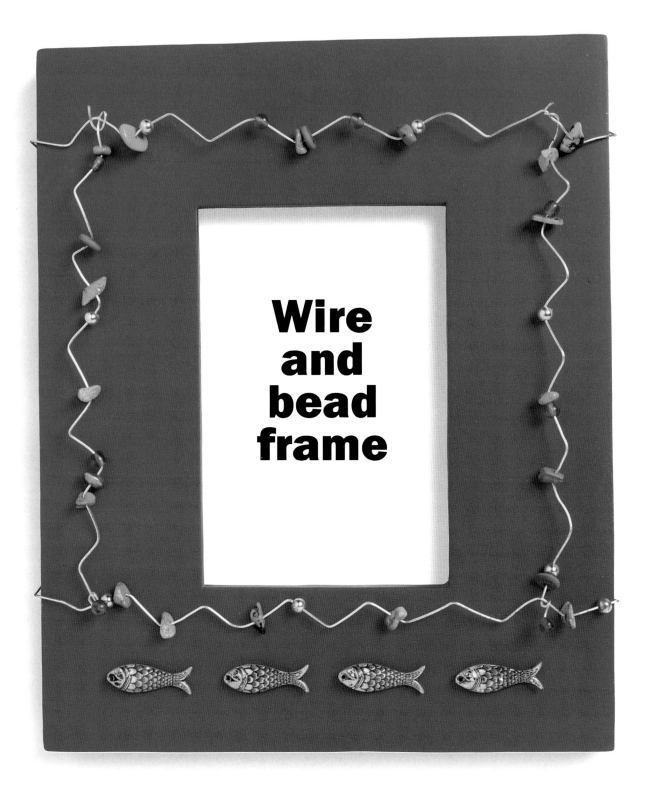

Wire
and
bead
frame

A delicate wave effect is created by fixing lengths of wire threaded with beads onto the front of this brightly coloured frame. The tiny fishes provide a charming additional decorative touch.

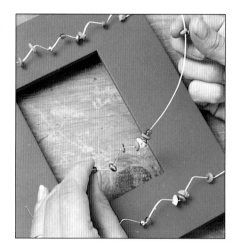

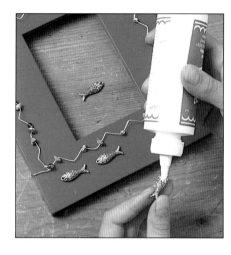

1 Apply the spray paint evenly to the frame. Be careful to do this in a well-ventilated room. Cut two pieces of wire of sufficient length to wrap around the top and bottom of the frame. Cut two shorter lengths of wire for the vertical decoration.

2 Thread the beads onto each of the longer pieces of wire and use pliers to bend into wave shapes, adjusting the positions of the beads as required. Wrap the decorated wire around the top and bottom borders of the frame. Twist the ends at the back of the frame to secure. Thread beads onto the shorter lengths of wire and bend in the same way. Attach these to the sides of the frame by bending the ends around the top and bottom wires.

3 Glue fishes and/or other small decorations along the bottom border.

Wire

Beads and tiny metal fishes

Round-nosed pliers

You will need

- Rectangular frame with wide, flat moulding
- 2 m (2¼ yards) of 10 mm (⅜ inch) wire
- Selection of beads and tiny metal fishes or other metal shapes that you can find in bead shops or make yourself from wire
- Pliers
- Bright blue spray paint
- PVA glue

Pretty paper

Paper, whether printed or patterned, provides one of the easiest methods of applying decoration to your frame surround. Whether you use the inherently attractive qualities of ready-made marbled paper or create patterns of your own in a collage of found paper items such as postcards or sheet music, paper decoration can produce a frame suitable for any occasion.

Quilled
frame

You will need

- Rectangular frame with flat moulding
- 3mm quilling paper in different colours
- PVA glue
- Quilling tool
- Tape measure or ruler
- Cocktail sticks
- Scissors

Book of quilling papers in different colours.

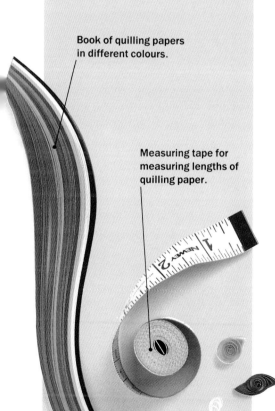

Measuring tape for measuring lengths of quilling paper.

Quilling is a wonderful way of creating your own scrolled paper decoration. Here the design is that of bright spring flowers. If you are new to the art of quilling, see Terms and techniques (pages 122–126).

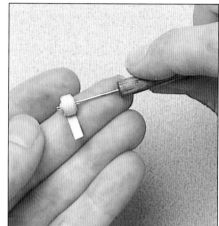

1 Roll 320 mm (12½ inches) of pink quilling paper firmly around the quilling tool. Allow the scroll to loosen slightly and glue the end to the outer edge. Apply the glue with a cocktail stick.

2 Pinch one side of the scroll to create a teardrop shape. Make a further nine teardrop shapes in the same way. Then make 20 smaller pink teardrops using 160-mm (6¼-inch) lengths of quilling paper and 20 from 80-mm (3⅛-inch) lengths. In addition, make 24 tight coils from 320-mm (12½-inch) lengths of yellow quilling paper.

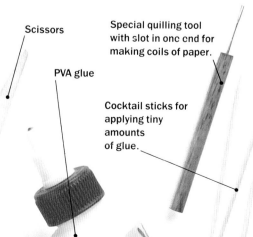

Scissors

Special quilling tool with slot in one end for making coils of paper.

PVA glue

Cocktail sticks for applying tiny amounts of glue.

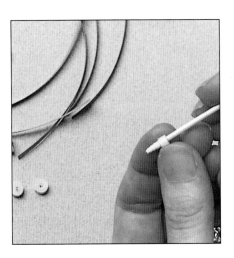

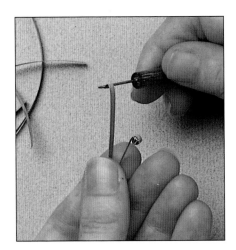

3 Using 160-mm (6¼-inch) lengths of yellow quilling paper, make 24 tight coils. After gluing, use a cocktail stick to push out the centres to make each coil into a horn shape.

4 Fold an 80-mm (3⅛-inch) length of green quilling paper in half to make a V shape. Make a scroll in each end. Make a total of 24 of these leaf shapes. In addition, make 24 similar V shapes from 30 mm (1⅛ inches) lengths of white quilling paper.

5 Glue each of the yellow flower coils into the V of each of the leaves. When dry, glue these together in groups of three to make eight triple flower heads. Then glue a white V shape into the centre of each yellow flower.

Simple shapes and colour schemes have been used for these quilled pieces which are made from loose coils and tight coils.

Quilling tool, similar to the one shown on the previous page. Alternatively, you can improvise by putting a dot of glue on the end of the quilling strip and wrapping it around a cocktail stick.

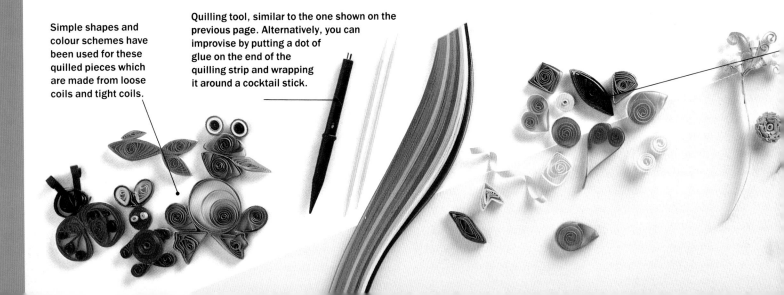

6 Assemble the pink teardrops in groups of five around a yellow coil centre to form pink flowers of different sizes and glue onto frame.

7 Glue an 80-mm (3⅛-inch) length of green quilling paper to the end of each flower head, and arrange these around the frame, interspersed with pink flowers. If desired, add leaves made from 160-mm (6¼-inch) lengths of green quilling paper formed into teardrop shapes.

8 Build up the pink flowers into a second layer using another central yellow coil and white bunny ears. When you are satisfied with the design, apply glue to the underside of the quilled elements and place them carefully into position on the frame. You could also make butterflies from blue and white coils and teardrop shapes.

Hearts, squares, lozenges, double scrolls – turn to page 126 for instructions on making different quilling shapes – then combine the different shapes to create a range of flower and leaf forms.

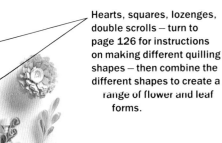

Finished frame
The frame can be left as it is here or sprayed with varnish.

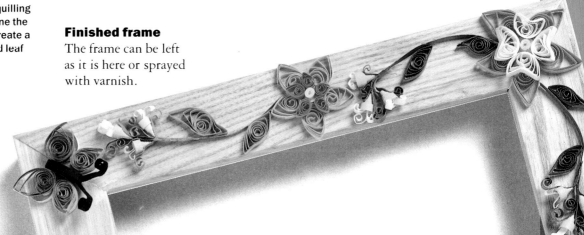

Multi-image frame

You will need

- Rectangular frame 250 × 300 mm/10 × 12 inches with flat front border approximately 65 mm (2½ inches) wide
- Four A4 photocopies of your chosen image(s)
- Wallpaper paste
- Ultramarine acrylic paint
- Clear polyurethane varnish (satin)
- Steel ruler
- Scissors
- Craft knife
- 25 mm (1 inch) and 12 mm (½ inch) flat paint brushes

The subtle effect of repeated images overlaid with a pale wash of colour is exemplified in this frame. There is plenty of scope for individual adaptation to suit the image to be framed in the choice of photocopied images and of colour.

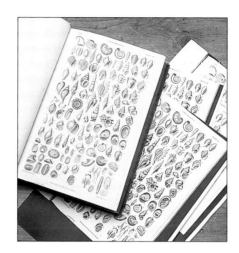 

1 Select a linear image – such as an engraving or line drawing to photocopy. In this example small drawings of shells, taken from Oliver Goldsmith's *A History of the Earth and Animated Nature* were used. Photocopy this four times onto A4 paper.

2 Cut the copies into pieces slightly larger than you need to cover the front of the frame. You will need to piece the sections together.

Jar of acrylic paint

Crumpled-up photocopies

12mm (½ inch) flat paint brush

Steel ruler

Craft knife

Cutting mat or use folded newspapers to protect your worktop when cutting.

Photocopies

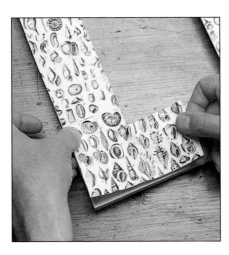

3 Screw up the cut-up photocopies and flatten them out again, being careful to avoid tearing the paper.

4 Apply wallpaper paste to the frame and photocopies. Place the copies in position around the frame. Butt up the different segments carefully so that the join is not visible. It doesn't matter if the photocopies hang over the edge of the frame.

5 When the frame is thoroughly dry, trim the excess paper on the inner and outer edges of the frame with a craft knife, using a steel ruler to provide a straight edge.

Inspiration for images to photocopy can be found in old botanical or zoological reference books.

Instead of photocopying images onto white paper, experiment with photocopying onto coloured paper.

Varnish for finishing the frame.

6 Using the smaller brush, paint the front of the frame with a very dilute wash of acrylic paint.

7 Make the colour more intense at the inner and outer edges by applying a second wash to these areas while the first is still wet.

8 Paint the inner and outer sides of the frame with full strength paint.

Finished frame Varnish was applied to the front and sides of the frame to protect and seal it.

Marbled paper frame

This stylish frame uses different types of marbled paper set off by a black-painted surround. You can make the marbled paper yourself, if you know how (there are many books available to show you) or you can buy a selection of ready-made papers from a craft supply shop.

1 Use a 25 mm (1 inch) brush to paint the outside edge of the frame with black acrylic paint.

2 While the paint is drying, cut the marbled paper into equal squares. Make the sides of the squares long enough to cover the width of the flat frame surround and wrap around the rebate. You need enough squares to cover the frame surround. Arrange the squares around the frame in pleasing colour combinations, alternating the different patterns.

3 Glue the squares to the frame with wallpaper paste and a 12 mm (½ inch) brush, working inwards from each corner. Make a small diagonal cut into the inner corner of each corner square to produce a neat finish. Adjust the width of the central square on each side to ensure an exact fit. When the paste is completely dry, polish the entire frame with furniture polish.

You will need

- Reverse moulding frame with flat surround
- At least four different kinds of marbled paper
- Wallpaper paste
- Black acrylic paint
- Craft knife

- Wax furniture polish, rag and polishing cloth
- Scissors
- Steel ruler
- 25 mm (1 inch) and 12 mm (½ inch) flat paint brushes

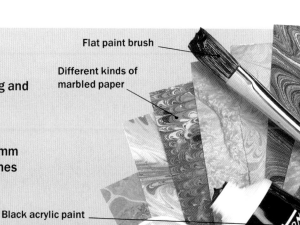

Flat paint brush

Different kinds of marbled paper

Black acrylic paint

Music lover's frame

This musical tribute in a frame can be used for a picture of a composer or perhaps of a musically inclined relative or friend. Use old sheet music, which can be obtained from second-hand bookshops and flea markets. Choose scores with plenty of visual, if not musical, interest.

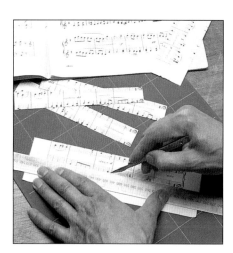

1 Paint the inner and outer mouldings with black acrylic paint, using a 12 mm (½ inch) brush. Use scissors or a craft knife to cut the music into strips, eliminating excess white paper between the staves.

2 Arrange the strips horizontally around the frame to fill the space between the inner and outer mouldings. Paste in position with the ends of the strips overlapping by about 1 cm (⅜ inch). Rub the paper with a finger to indicate the exact cut-off line. Trim with scissors and tap down paper.

3 Allow the paste to dry. Tint the varnish with a little Burnt Sienna oil paint, using a 5 mm squeeze of paint to about 10 mm of varnish in a jar. Apply this to the entire frame with a 25 mm (1 inch) brush. This gives a pleasingly "aged" effect to the music.

You will need

- Frame with wide reverse moulding
- Old sheet music
- Wallpaper paste
- Black acrylic paint
- Burnt Sienna oil paint
- Clear polyurethane satin-finish varnish

- Fine glasspaper
- Craft knife
- Scissors
- Steel ruler
- 25 mm (1 inch) and 12 mm (½ inch) flat paint brushes

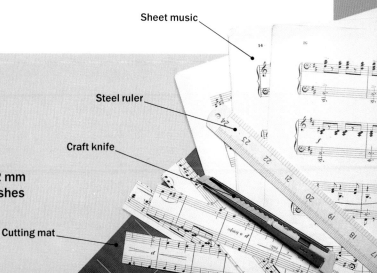

Sheet music

Steel ruler

Craft knife

Cutting mat

Matisse-inspired frame

This simple but colourful frame uses découpage — the technique of decorating surfaces with shapes cut from paper. The design is inspired by the work of the painter Henri Matisse, leader of the Fauves, known for their extravagant use of colour.

1 Cut out pieces of paper in various colours, leaving an overlap to wrap behind the frame. Position the paper round the frame as required and paste down, spreading paste on both paper and frame. Using the tips of your fingers, smooth out any bubbles, taking care not to tear the paper.

2 Paste dark-coloured paper around the inner rim, smoothing down as you go. Mitre the corners by eye, making sure that all small pieces are stuck firmly.

3 Using a template, cut leaf shapes out of the remaining coloured paper. Paste the leaves onto the frame, contrasting the colour of the leaves with the colour blocks already pasted. Cut out thin strips of paper and, again using contrasting colours, paste these onto the centre of the leaves to look like veins. Leave the frame to dry and then apply the varnish.

Sheets of brightly coloured thin paper

Scissors

Pasting brush

You will need

- A frame with a flat wide surround
- Assorted sheets of brightly coloured thin paper
- Cellulose (wallpaper) paste

- Brush for pasting
- Scissors
- Polyurethane varnish

Wallpaper paste

Postcard
frame

You will need

- Frame with flat surround
- Old postcards
- Wallpaper paste
- Pale yellow acrylic paint
- Clear polyurethane satin-finish varnish
- Fine glasspaper
- Craft knife
- Scissors
- Steel ruler
- 50 mm (2 inch) and 25 mm (1 inch) flat paint brushes

Old postcards

Utilize the decorative potential of old postcards to create this nostalgic frame. If you don't have your own collection, you can often buy these cheaply in flea markets and bric-a-brac shops. Select cards with interesting stamps and attractive handwriting.

1 Arrange the postcards around the frame. In this example, most of the cards are placed writing side uppermost, with small areas of black and white images from the cards used to provide contrast in the gaps. Place the postcards at an angle to the frame edge and be sure to butt the edges close up to each other. Take time to ensure a pleasing effect. When you are satisfied with the arrangement of the cards, bend over overlapping edges and those that extend beyond the frame edge with a finger.

2 Start to paste them onto the frame one-by-one, trimming as you go. Apply wallpaper paste to the frame and to the back of the card and replace the card in position.

Steel ruler – an ideal tool for providing a clean straight edge.

Scissors

Craft knife

Flat paint brushes

Yellow acrylic paint

Satin-finish varnish

Glasspaper

Victorian découpage frame This style of frame evokes the superb collage style popular in the 19th century. The selection of romantic figures and flower images is a key part of the frame's appeal.

3 When the paste is dry, smooth the rough edges with glasspaper.

4 Paint the inner and outer edges of the frame with pale yellow acrylic paint, using a 25 mm (1 inch) brush.

Finished frame When the paint was dry, a coat of varnish was applied to the frame to protect and seal it.

Cartoon-character frame Ideal for a child's bedroom, this frame is decorated with cartoon characters cut out from comics. Those that break out of the frame are backed with card before being glued onto the frame.

Glittering sweet-wrap frame This glitzy frame uses a collage of shiny sweet wrappers. Try out this idea with papers of all colours or limit your "palette" to create a more restrained effect.

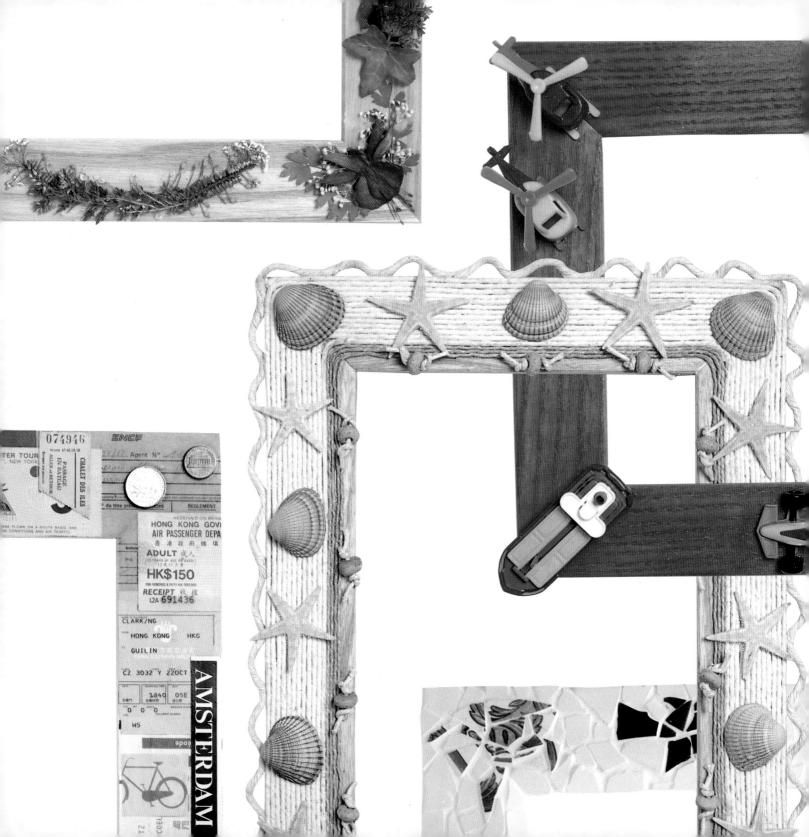

Fortunate finds

Every home is a treasure chest for the frame decorator. Whether you look in the pantry or toy box, tool shed or garden, you will find a host of tiny objects that can be glued to a plain or painted frame to create a highly individual effect.

Woodland frame

You will need

- Frame with wide flat moulding
- Selection of barks, berries, cones, leaves, etc.
- PVA glue
- Craft knife

A *woodland walk can provide a wealth of free materials for this nature-lover's frame. Collect berries, bark, cones, nuts, leaves and so on. You will need to dry berries by hanging them in a warm place for a few days. Press leaves between paper under a heavy book.*

1 Dry out berries, fungi and bark in a warm place to ensure they don't turn mouldy. For leaves use a flower press or place between sheets of paper under a heavy book.

2 Trim the bark into small pieces. Arrange them around the frame, alternating different colours and textures, and overlapping the edges to create an interesting effect. Glue to the frame.

Selection of barks, berries, cones, leaves, funghi

PVA glue

Craft knife

Beachcomber frame
Here a collection of items found on a stroll along a beach makes a bold frame for a seaside holiday cottage.

3 Take a selection of berries, nuts and other items you have collected, and arrange these around the frame to enhance the effect. Some items may need to be trimmed to fit.

4 Carefully stick each element onto the frame one at a time.

Finished frame This design is perfect for displaying a single pressed leaf or a beautifully handwritten poem with an autumn theme.

Lobster pot frame A painted blue lobster made from a wire armature covered with papier mâché is a delightful cornerpiece for this driftwood frame. Insert a mirror to make a "pool of water" in the centre of the frame.

Driftwood frame
Fragments of sea-weathered driftwood glued to a plain frame base achieve an unexpectedly harmonious result.

China
mosaic
frame

You will need

- Rectangular frame with flat moulding
- Glazed tiles or pottery of approximately the same thickness in shades of blue and white
- PVA glue
- Ready-mixed all-purpose white grout
- Safety glasses
- Hammer
- Pliers
- Pencil
- Wooden work-surface such as a large chopping board
- Sponge
- Putty knife

*R*eminiscent of the mosaic work of the Classical world, you can adapt this method of frame decoration to depict the motifs of your choice using appropriate colours.

1 Draw your design in pencil onto the front of the frame. Images of fish and other sea creatures have been selected here.

2 Wearing the safety glasses to prevent fragments flying into the eyes, use the hammer to break up the tiles/pottery into small pieces – approximately 6–12 mm (¼–½ inch) across. Work on a solid wooden surface. Save time on sorting the pieces by breaking up items of the same colour together.

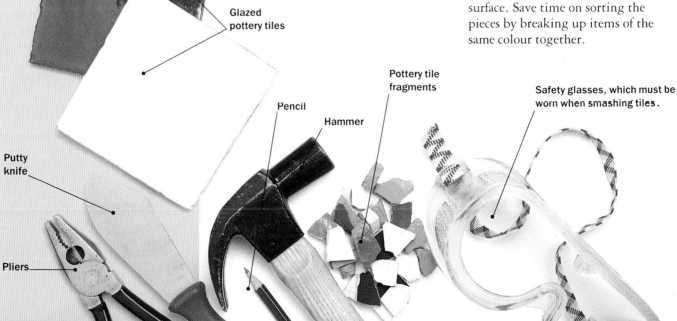

Glazed pottery tiles

Pottery tile fragments

Pencil

Hammer

Safety glasses, which must be worn when **smashing tiles**.

Putty knife

Pliers

3 Use a pair of pliers to break off any rough edges.

4 Decide which colours you will use for each motif. Start to stick down pieces of pottery in the planned positions. Allow a gap of about 3 mm (⅛ inch) between the pieces. Complete a small area at a time.

5 When the design is complete and the frame is completely covered by your mosaic, allow the glue to dry for at least 24 hours.

Glass fragments can be used instead of china for creating a mosaic effect. Handle with care!

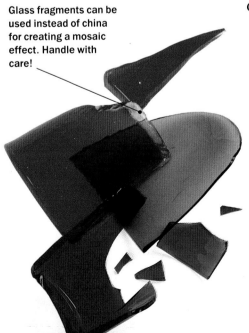

Never throw away broken crockery. Recycle it!

6 When the glue is thoroughly dry, fill the gaps between the pottery pieces with grout. Press the grout down into the gaps, filling to the level of the pieces.

7 Wipe the excess grout from the surface of the mosaic using a damp sponge. Be careful to remove all traces of grout while it is still wet; it is difficult to clean off once it is dry. It is best to fill and wipe away in small sections to prevent the grout drying too soon. Allow the grout to dry thoroughly as specified in the manufacturer's instructions.

Unglazed broken terracotta pots can be used to good effect.

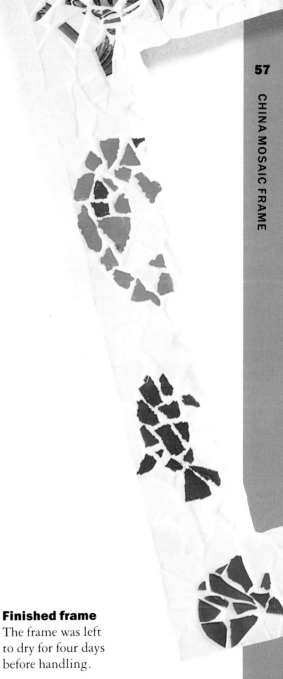

Finished frame
The frame was left to dry for four days before handling.

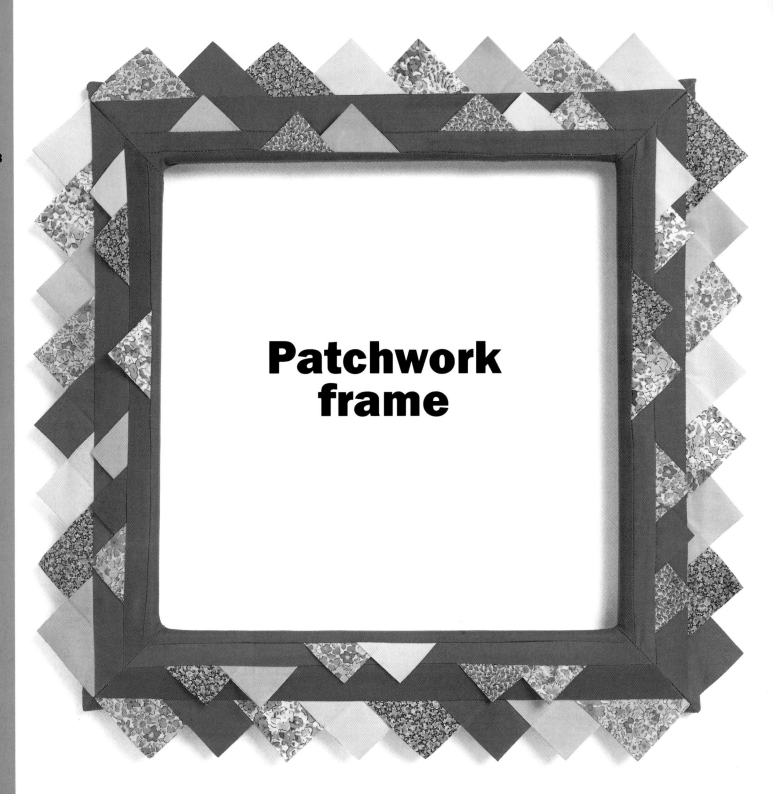

Patchwork
frame

You will need

- Square frame with flat-fronted reverse moulding approximately 50 mm (2 inches) wide
- Selection of lightweight fabrics – eg four prints and three plains
- Toning thread
- Bondaweb
- Double-sided adhesive tape
- Paper for templates
- Scissors
- Fabric tacking stick
- Tape measure or ruler
- Sewing machine
- Iron and ironing board

An imaginative way to use all those tiny offcuts of fabric in your sewing basket, this frame evokes memories of childhood, with its pretty floral prints worked into a Prairie Points patchwork design.

1 Make paper templates for each of the triangle points. Use large triangles for decorating the outer edge of the frame and smaller ones for the centre and inner edges. Position these around the frame.

2 When you are satisfied with the number and position of the triangles, make up the triangles in fabric. Iron strips of hemming web into the folds to provide rigidity to thin fabrics.

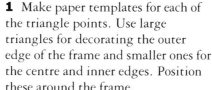

Tape measure

Glue stick

Double-sided adhesive tape

Selection of lightweight fabrics: choose colours that contrast or co-ordinate.

Thread to match fabrics

Scissors

Iron, for use with iron-on webbing.

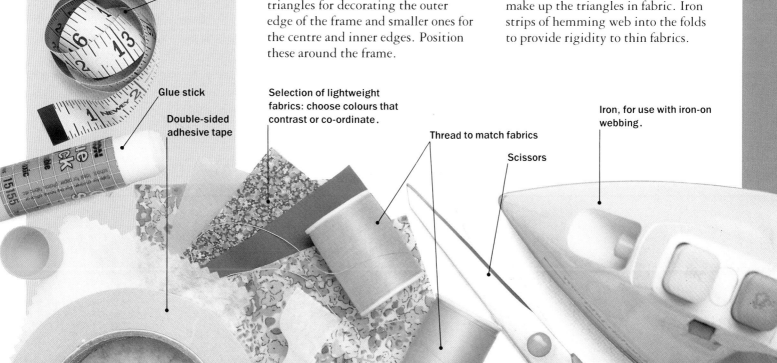

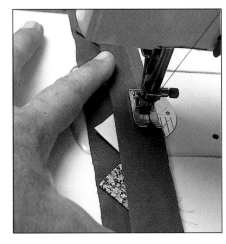

3 Cut four sets of fabric strips to cover the frame. Make sure that the outer and inner strips are wide enough to wrap around the outer and inner edges of the frame. Take one of the outer strips and starting from the centre, place the planned number of larger triangles along the cut edge of the strip. When they are correctly positioned, secure with tack stick.

4 Machine stitch the next strip in place, concealing the bases of the triangles. Iron flat. Arrange the smaller triangles in their planned positions along the inner edge of the next strip, remembering that this strip will be slightly shorter than the outer one because of the mitre.

5 Repeat the process for the third strip. The final strip has no triangles attached. Complete three more pieces for the remaining sides of the frame in the same way.

Pinking shears for finishing the edges of fabric.

Choose thread that co-ordinates with the fabric you are using.

For a patchwork effect, simply cover the frame in fabric, then stick on overlapping fabric squares with pinked edges.

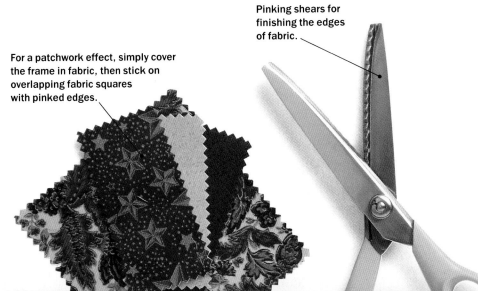

6 Join the sections for each side by stitching a mitred seam. Make sure that the end triangles on the outer strips touch those on the adjacent strip.

7 Place lengths of double-sided tape around the back of the frame and on the frame front. Position the patchwork over the frame. Match the mitres of the frame to those of the sewn fabric. Wrap the outer edges around the frame, being careful to keep the points level and the corners neat. Press onto the tape at the back of the frame to secure.

8 Turn the frame over and place double-sided tape along the rebate. Pull the inner edges taut and press onto the tape to secure to the rebate.

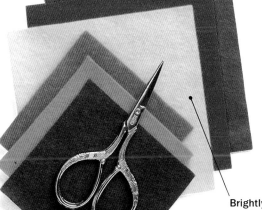

Brightly coloured felt can also be used to create a patchwork effect.

Finished frame
The frame was complete once stray threads were trimmed away from the front of the frame.

Ribbon-weave frame

This sumptuous frame utilizes the rich colours and textures of ribbon. Vary the effect by choosing different colourways and patterns to match the image you intend to frame.

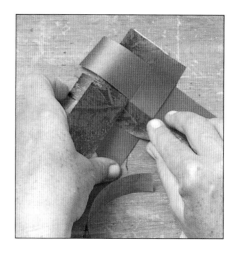

1 Select different ribbons to run along the length of each side of the frame. The combined width of each set of ribbons should be sufficient to cover the frame front. Cut the ribbons to the length of the frame plus twice the frame depth.

2 Cut four pieces of iron-on interfacing to the exact width of the four sides of the frame front and the same length as the ribbons. Lay the first set of ribbons over a piece of interfacing and iron the ends to secure in place.

3 Take the next set of ribbons and weave these through the first set, alternately "over and under" and "under and over". Leave about 10 mm (⅜ inch) protruding at one side.

You will need

- **Square frame with curved reverse moulding approximately 65 mm (2½ inches) wide**
- **Selection of ribbons in different widths and colours**
- **Lightweight iron-on interfacing (Vilene)**

- **Double-sided adhesive tape**
- **Craft knife**
- **Scissors**
- **Ruler**
- **Iron and ironing board**

Ribbons in co-ordinating colours and different widths

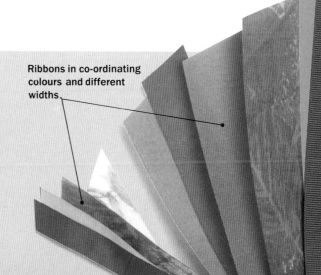

4 Cut lots of lengths of ribbon of different colours, widths and types to the width of the frame plus the depth of the frame and rebate. Weave these through the first set of ribbons for the length of the frame opening, allowing the loose ends to protrude equally at each side. Finish with a further set of long ribbons.

5 Secure the weave by ironing the ribbons onto the interfacing. Fix a second piece of interfacing at right angles to the first to start the second side of the frame.

6 Weave more short ribbons into the next set of long ribbons. Weave the final set of long ribbons to finish this side and to form the basis of the third side. Iron the ribbons onto the interfacing and attach the next piece as before. Continue to work until you have completed all four sides, checking from time to time that the weaving fits the frame correctly. Make sure that the alternating "under and over" sequence is correct on the fourth side where it meets the first.

Tiny ready-made bows and rosebuds, available from haberdashers, for putting the finishing touches to fabric-covered frames.

Metallic threads and embroidery threads. Thicker metallic threads can be used for weaving or winding round a frame; thinner threads can be used for embroidery.

Thick yarns in assorted colours can be used instead of ribbons for weaving.

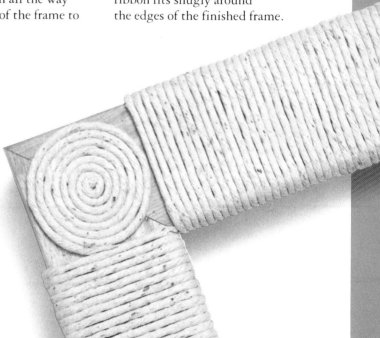

7 Place strips of double-sided tape around the outer edge of the frame and on the frame front. Carefully lay the woven ribbon onto the frame so that the loose ends of the short ribbons overlap the inner and outer edges of the frame. Press into position to secure the weave to the front and outer edge of the frame. Turn the frame over and place double-sided tape on the rebate. Press the loose ribbons on the inner edge under the rebate to secure.

8 Use double-sided tape to secure a length of toning ribbon all the way around the outer edge of the frame to provide a neat finish.

Finished frame The woven ribbon fits snugly around the edges of the finished frame.

String-bound frame As easy as you could wish – this natural coloured frame is simply bound with string. Coiled decorations embellish the corners.

String frame

String is available in a wonderful variety of colours and textures that can be used to create original decorative effects. Try twisting, coiling and layering the string to produce a variety of different designs.

 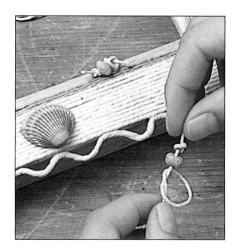 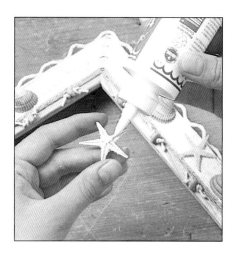

1 Apply glue to the front of the frame. Stick the medium string all the way round the outer edge of the front of the frame. Continue working inwards until you have made a border covering approximately three quarters the width of the frame. Make sure that you stick the string neatly into each corner. Apply a thin line of glue to the outer edge of the frame. Stick a wavy line of thick string around the frame.

2 Glue several rows of fine brown string inside the medium string border, leaving an inside edge of approximately 3 mm (⅛ inch) bare. Thread small shells onto lengths of brown string and knot at each end to secure. Glue these onto the bare wood along the inside edge.

3 Finish by gluing shells and starfish to the string-decorated frame front. Be careful not to create an overcrowded effect.

Different types of string

PVA glue

Seashore finds

 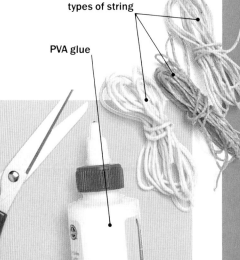

You will need

- Rectangular frame with flat moulding
- Selection of different types of string – thick, medium, fine brown, fine white

- Shells, pebbles, starfish or other seashore items
- Scissors
- PVA glue

Scissors

Pressed flowers frame

*Create the impression of a summer garden with this delightfully
fresh decorative idea. Choose flowers of toning colours such as
the shades of purple and lavender shown here.*

1 Pick the flowers and leaves at a time when they are dry from dew or rain. Press them between layers of absorbent paper (blotting paper, paper handkerchiefs or kitchen roll) for about six weeks. Always press more than you think you will need.

2 Using tweezers to pick them up, arrange the flowers and leaves around the front of the frame. It is effective to arrange the leaves in a background design first, and to position the flowers at key points later. Carefully apply a small amount of glue to the backs of the leaves using a cocktail stick and fix in position on the frame. Allow to dry for about 30 minutes.

3 Stick sprigs of dried Gypsophilia to the corners of frame in the same way, if desired. Stick some of the larger flowers in each corner over the Gypsophilia to produce a "button hole" effect. Stick smaller flowers individually or on stems around the frame. Trim the stalks with scissors as necessary. Allow to dry for 24 hours before further handling.

You will need

- Rectangular frame with flat moulding
- Flower press or heavy books
- Selection of fresh flowers and leaves

- PVA glue
- Tweezers
- Scissors
- Cocktail sticks
- Absorbent paper

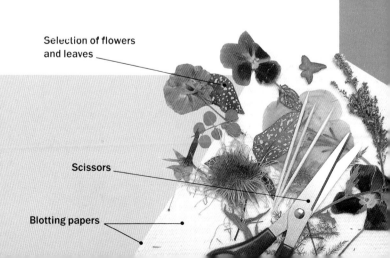

Selection of flowers and leaves

Scissors

Blotting papers

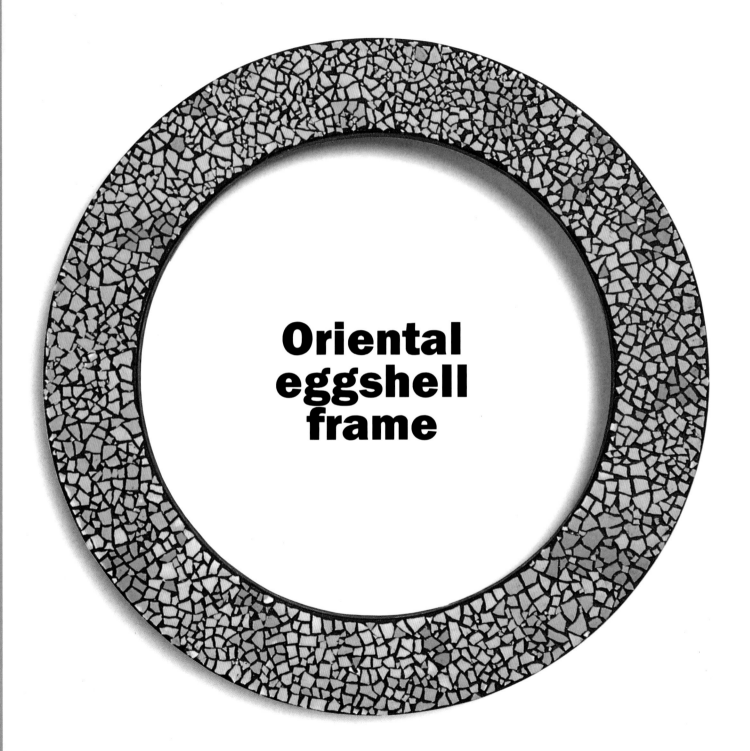

Oriental eggshell frame

The restrained crackled effect of this frame would be an ideal complement to a sparse modern interior. Use it for a sepia photo portrait or a simple line drawing or silhouette.

1 Seal the frame with shellac or other sealant. When dry, sand lightly. Apply three coats of black paint to the front and sides of the frame, allowing it to dry between coats.

2 Burnish the frame after the final coat with wire wool to obtain a silky finish.

3 Crack the eggs and discard the contents. Carefully separate the outer shells from the membrane that lines them. This is best done as soon as the eggs are cracked open while the membrane is still damp and pliable.

You will need

- 180 mm (7 inch) diameter circular frame with flat moulding
- 3–4 eggs – preferably with white or pale brown shells
- Black casein-based hobby paint or black emulsion
- PVA wood glue
- Matt varnish

- Fine grade wire wool
- Shellac (or sanding sealer)
- Greaseproof paper
- Round pencil or length of dowel
- Fine-grade wet and dry glasspaper
- Paint brush
- Craft knife

Glasspaper

Circular frame with flat moulding

Fine grade wire wool

Shells from 3–4 eggs

Greaseproof paper

Length of dowel

Craft knife

PVA wood glue

4 Break off a piece of eggshell about the size of a fingernail and use a fine paint brush to apply glue to the inside of the shell.

5 Place the glued shell glue-side down onto the frame. Cover with a piece of greaseproof paper and roll the pencil or dowel across the shell to break it into smaller pieces

6 Working quickly with the point of a craft knife before the glue dries, start sliding the small pieces of shell apart, to reveal some negative space between them. Continue in this way until the whole frame is covered. To ensure complete coverage of the frame front allow the pieces of shell to overlap the edges.

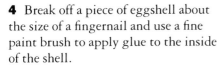
For a bold effect, try eggshells painted in bright primaries using food colours or acrylic paints.

Eggshells sprayed gold for a rich effect.

Acrylic paints dry hard and bright — perfect for painting eggshells — and the colours aren't fugitive, which means they don't fade.

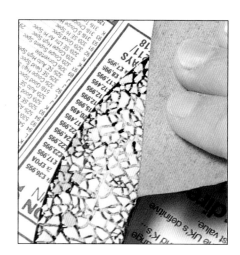

7 When the glue is completely dry, turn the frame face down and trim off excess shell that is overlapping the edges with a sharp craft knife.

8 Apply six coats of varnish, allowing each to dry before applying the next. After the sixth coat sand the frame with wetted wet and dry glasspaper in a circular motion. Wipe the resultant "sludge" from the frame with a clean, damp cloth and allow to dry before applying another coat of varnish. Continue to build up coats of varnish in this way until the shell fragments no longer stand proud of the frame surface. Do not sand the final coat of varnish.

Quails' eggs left in their natural speckled state.

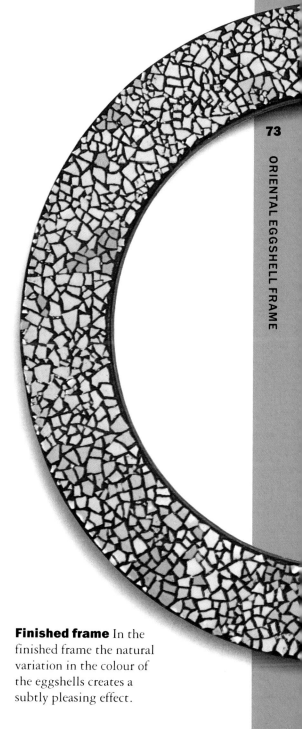

Finished frame In the finished frame the natural variation in the colour of the eggshells creates a subtly pleasing effect.

Seeds
frame

This frame decorated with dried pulses and seeds commonly found in the kitchen cupboard is a marvellously striking design. Choose materials with dramatically contrasting colours, as in this example, or vary the effect by selecting more muted shades.

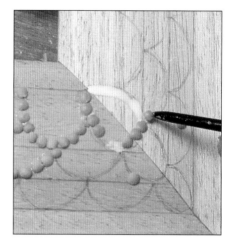

1 Seal the frame with shellac or an alternative sealer and sand lightly when dry to remove the raised grain. Measure and draw the outline of the arch design in pencil. Rule guidelines on the frame front to help you to draw arches of a consistent height.

2 Apply glue along a small area of the design at a time, using a fine paintbrush.

3 Stick lentils along the glued line, flat side down. Slide them into place using the wrong end of a paint brush. Butt the lentils up closely, pressing down to secure. Continue until all the lines are covered.

Rectangular frame
with reverse moulding

Shellac, a traditional lacquer
used to give a lustrous finish.

Selection of seeds
and pulses

Flat varnish brush

Ruler

You will need

- Rectangular frame with reverse moulding
- 1 cup of orange split lentils
- 1 cup of yellow split peas
- 4 sunflower seeds
- 1 cup of tiny black seeds such as poppy or mustard seeds
- Shellac (or sanding sealer)

- PVA wood glue
- Varnish
- Pencil
- Ruler
- Greaseproof paper
- Small brush for glue
- Cheap brush for Shellac (clean in methylated spirits)
- 25 mm (1 inch) flat varnish brush

Pencil

4 Stick the peas, also flat side down, along the outside and inside edges of the frame. Place a sunflower seed at each inside corner.

5 Use the black seeds to fill in all the rest of the background. Apply glue to a small area at a time.

6 Sprinkle a generous pinch of seeds onto the glued area.

The kitchen cupboard will yield up all sorts of items that could be used to make a frame similar to the one shown in this project.

Finished frame
The deep gloss
finish of the final
frame enhances the
richness of the
colours.

7 Cover the area with greaseproof
paper and press down firmly.
Continue in this way until the entire
frame is covered. Once the glue is
dry, tip the frame on its side to allow
excess or unglued seeds to fall off.
Patch any areas that are insufficiently
covered.

8 Carefully apply a thick coat of
varnish, using a wide, flat brush.
Avoid overbrushing, which may
dislodge small seeds. Apply a further
three to five coats of varnish, allowing
the frame to dry between coats.

Domino
frame

The simple idea of applying domino pieces to a flat-fronted frame creates a stunning effect. The red-painted frame edges provide a discreet accent to the black and white decoration. This frame would complement any modern office or home.

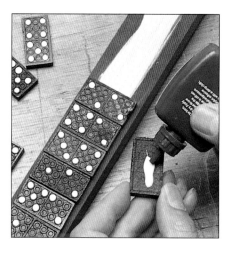

1 Paint the outside and inside edges of the frame with red acrylic paint. Then paint a 1 cm (⅜ inch) border on both edges of the front surround.

2 Arrange the dominoes around the frame, so that the different dot combinations form a pleasing effect.

3 Stick the dominoes to the frame making sure that the red border shows along the edges of the frame.

You will need

- Frame (200 × 300 mm/8 × 12 inches) with flat surround approximately 45 mm (1¾ inches) wide
- Approximately 38 dominoes
- PVA wood glue
- Red acrylic paint
- 12 mm (½ inch) flat paint brush

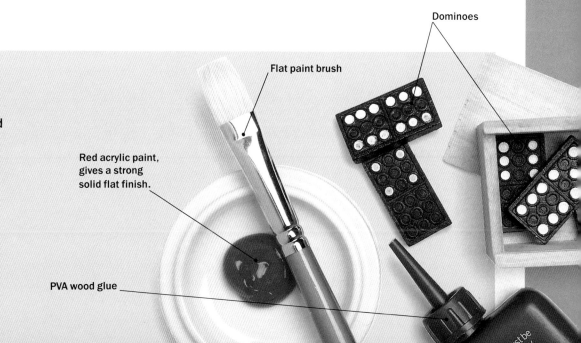

Dominoes

Flat paint brush

Red acrylic paint, gives a strong solid flat finish.

PVA wood glue

Toy
frame

Ideal for framing a picture or mirror for a child's room, this simple technique can be used with any small toys. The stained wood background that shows the grain, sets off the bright primary colours of the toys.

1 Rub down the frame with glasspaper to achieve a smooth surface. Apply wood stain according to the manufacturer's instructions, using as many coats as necessary to gain the depth of colour you want.

2 When the stain is dry, place the toys around the frame, experimenting with their positions until you find the most pleasing arrangement. When you are happy with the effect, lightly mark the contact points of the toys on the frame in pencil.

3 Working on a few at a time, stick the toys to the frame in the marked positions, following the manufacturer's instructions for the adhesive. Allow the glue to harden for at least 24 hours before moving the frame.

You will need

- Rectangular frame with flat moulding approximately 35mm (1¼ inches) wide
- Selection of small, light toys
- Pencil
- Wood stain
- Fine glasspaper
- Impact adhesive
- Rubber gloves

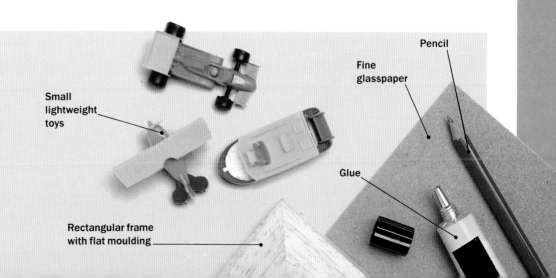

Pencil

Fine glasspaper

Small lightweight toys

Glue

Rectangular frame with flat moulding

Folk art frame

This delightful decorative idea, inspired by European and American folk art, can be adapted to use different types of small wooden or plastic animals and figures. The natural colours selected for the frame add to the traditional effect.

1 Paint the front of the frame in terracotta acrylic paint. Then paint the inside and outside edges of the frame in green.

2 Trim the bases from the animals, if they have them, and arrange the pieces around the frame in a decorative fashion.

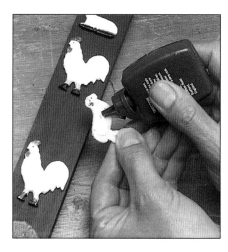

3 Use PVA wood glue to stick the animals to the frame.

You will need

- Frame (300 × 400 mm/12 × 16 inches) with flat surround approximately 45 mm (1¾ inches) wide
- Flat wooden or plastic figures
- PVA wood glue
- Terracotta and green acrylic paints
- 25 mm (1 inch) flat paint brush
- Hacksaw

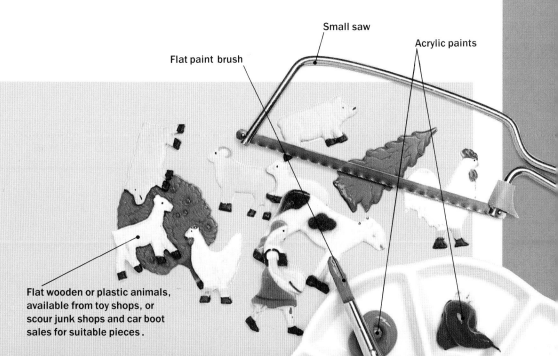

Flat paint brush

Small saw

Acrylic paints

Flat wooden or plastic animals, available from toy shops, or scour junk shops and car boot sales for suitable pieces.

Holiday
memento
frame

Here is a superb idea for framing a holiday photograph at the same time as displaying those evocative pieces of holiday memorabilia. Tickets, receipts, café matchbooks, hotel stationery – keep them all for creating this very special frame.

1 Arrange the mementos around the frame. Some items may need to be trimmed to fit and to create more interesting shapes. Allowing the different elements to overlap produces a pleasing effect.

2 Carefully stick each element onto the frame one at a time.

3 When the glue is completely dry, turn the frame over and trim away any paper that is overlapping with a craft knife. Apply two coats of varnish to the front and outside edges of the frame, allowing the varnish to dry between coats.

Holiday memorabilia: currency, stamps, bus tickets, and so on.

Craft knife

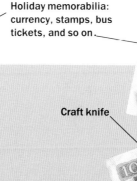

You will need

- Frame with flat moulding
- Selection of holiday mementos (tickets, foreign currency, packaging, menus, etc)
- White acrylic paint

- PVA glue
- Craft knife
- Scissors
- Clear matt varnish
- 12 mm (½ inch) flat paint brush

PVA glue

Into the third dimension

Use your frame as a base for sculptured relief in gesso and papier mâché, or by building on other materials such as string. You can also change the shape of the frame by adding a cardboard surround. Relief work can be painted or gilded according to the effect you want.

Gesso and gilded frame

*C*onjure up the atmosphere of a Renaissance interior with this heavy
gilded frame complete with "architectural" moulding. Use it to set off a
reproduction of an old oil painting or mirror.

1 Stick the two pieces of card together with PVA glue. Place the frame face down on the cardboard, allowing sufficient margins on all sides to accommodate the intended shape of the finished moulding. Draw around the inside and outside edges. Remove the frame and increase the size of the central hole by 12 mm (½ inch) all around. Draw the shape of the new frame on the cardboard.

2 Using a craft knife and a steel rule to ensure straight edges, cut the shapes out of the cardboard.

3 Apply glue to the front of the original frame and place the cardboard surround on top, making sure that an equal margin of the inner edge of the frame shows around the central hole. Place the frame and surround face down on a hard surface and weight with a heavy book until the glue is dry.

Gilt cream, available from
art materials suppliers.

You will need

- Rectangular frame with flat moulding
- 2 sheets of cardboard 85 mm (3½ inches) longer and 25 mm (1 inch) wider than the frame
- PVA glue

- Papier mâché pulp (see Recipes, page 125)
- Gesso (see Recipes, page 125)
- Reddish brown emulsion paint
- Gilt cream
- Pencil

- White spirit or turpentine
- 25 mm (1 inch) flat brush
- Round bristle brush
- Steel ruler
- Craft knife
- Soft cloths

Soft cloth for
applying gilt cream.

4 Apply a layer of papier mâché pulp to the frame front, pressing it into the inner edges of frame. Smooth flat. Roll out sausage shapes and arrange these around the outer edges of the surround. Carefully smooth the relief shapes onto the background layer of pulp. Add further decoration made from round balls of pulp. Leave to dry overnight in a warm place such as an airing cupboard.

5 When the frame is thoroughly dry, apply at least three coats of gesso, allowing the frame to dry between coats. Paint the whole frame, including the wooden sides, with reddish brown emulsion. Allow to dry.

6 Apply gilt cream to the frame with a soft cloth. When dry, buff with a clean, soft cloth to a high lustre.

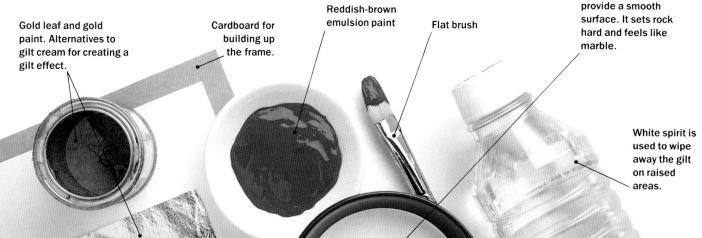

Gold leaf and gold paint. Alternatives to gilt cream for creating a gilt effect.

Cardboard for building up the frame.

Reddish-brown emulsion paint

Flat brush

Gesso is used to provide a smooth surface. It sets rock hard and feels like marble.

White spirit is used to wipe away the gilt on raised areas.

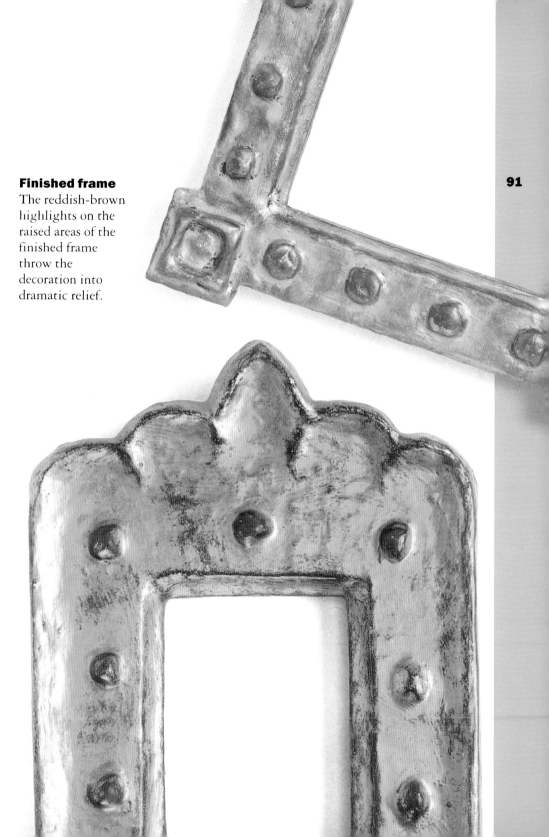

Finished frame
The reddish-brown highlights on the raised areas of the finished frame throw the decoration into dramatic relief.

7 To give an authentic antique look, dampen a clean, soft cloth in white spirit – do not soak it – and carefully wipe the gilt on raised areas to reveal the undercoat.

Medieval frame
This frame, constructed in the same way as the main project, conjures up images of stone castles and dark candlelit interiors.

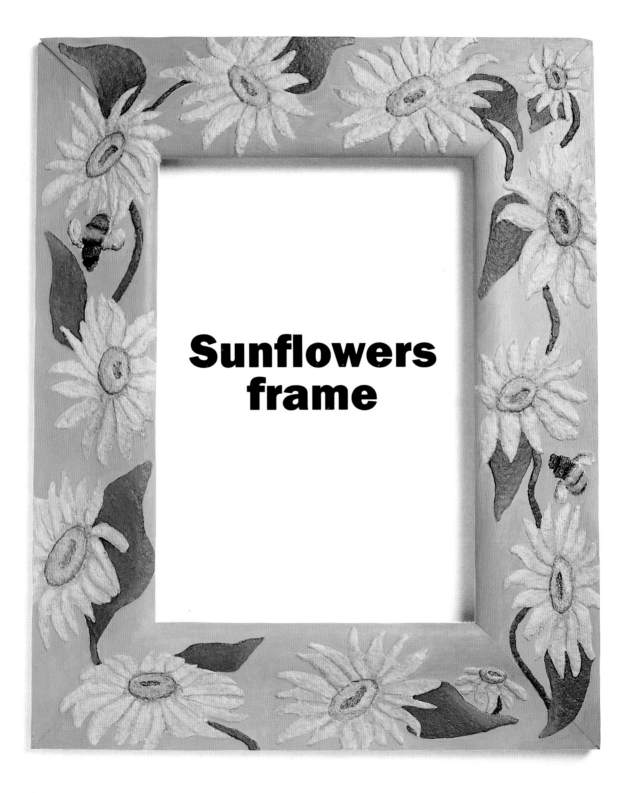

Sunflowers frame

You will need

- Rectangular frame with curved reverse moulding approximately 100 mm (4 inches) wide
- About 10 sheets of newspaper torn into small squares
- Interior filler (powder form)
- White emulsion paint
- Acrylic paints (greens, yellow, black)
- PVA glue
- Bucket
- Hand blender
- Modelling tools
- Sieve
- Small sponge
- Paint brushes

Fill your home with sunshine with this frame embellished with a relief decoration of sunflowers, foliage and bees made from paper pulp. You can adapt this versatile technique to create virtually any motif of your choice.

1 Put the torn newspaper into the bucket and pour over sufficient boiling water to cover. Leave to soak for about two hours.

2 Use the blender to chop the soaked paper to a pulp. Do this in short bursts to avoid overheating the blender. You may need to add more hot water as you work. Be sure to pulp all the paper.

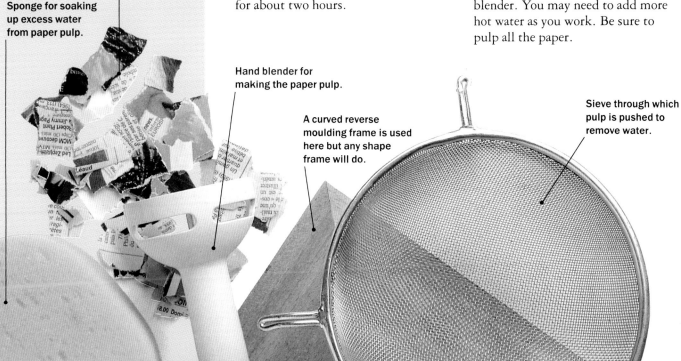

Torn newspaper

Sponge for soaking up excess water from paper pulp.

Hand blender for making the paper pulp.

A curved reverse moulding frame is used here but any shape frame will do.

Sieve through which pulp is pushed to remove water.

3 Strain the paper pulp through the sieve to remove excess water. Add three tablespoons of interior filler and two tablespoons of PVA glue to the pulp. Mix thoroughly.

4 Draw the outline of the flowers and other design elements in pencil on the frame. Working on a small area at a time, apply PVA glue inside the drawn shapes.

5 Mould the pulp to form the approximate relief shapes of the petals and other elements and place the pulp shapes in the glued positions. As you work, dab the pulp shapes with a sponge to remove any excess water.

Paper pulp

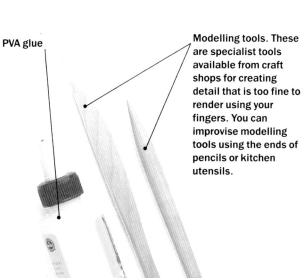

PVA glue

Modelling tools. These are specialist tools available from craft shops for creating detail that is too fine to render using your fingers. You can improvise modelling tools using the ends of pencils or kitchen utensils.

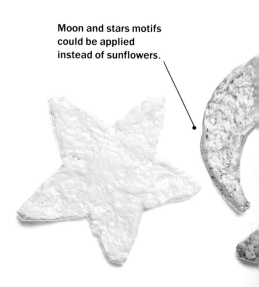

Moon and stars motifs could be applied instead of sunflowers.

6 Use the modelling tools to work the rough shapes into the precise shapes you want. Make the petals thinner at the ends for a more realistic three-dimensional effect. When you are satisfied with the effect, paint a finishing layer of diluted PVA glue over the area for extra hardness. Place the frame overnight in a warm place.

7 When the pulp decoration is completely dry and hard to the touch, apply two coats of white emulsion to the whole frame, allowing it to dry between coats.

8 When the undercoat is quite dry, paint the frame and the relief decoration in the colours shown.

Finished frame The careful choice of colours for the finished frame is the key element in creating a successful final effect.

Cherub frame

This antique-style frame, complete with baroque cherub, is a fitting embellishment for an old mirror. Decorate the frame with just one figure, or place one at each corner to create an even more lavish effect.

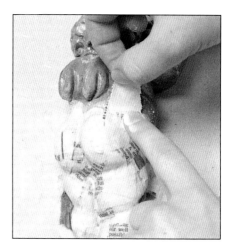

1 Working on the board, model the cherub shape of your choice from the clay. Try to make strong shapes as detail may be lost in the papier mâché. Do not undercut the edges of the figure where it meets the board, because this makes later removal of the papier mâché difficult. Let dry.

2 Make approximately one cup paste for the papier mâché by mixing flour and water to the consistency of thick cream. Add one tablespoonful of PVA glue to the paste. Make more paste later if you need it. Coat the cherub with petroleum jelly or cooking oil.

3 Dip each square of newspaper into the paste, wiping off any excess, and place onto the clay cherub. Overlap the paper squares as you work. Continue until the cherub is completely covered with a layer of paper. Allow to dry, before starting on the next layer. In this way, build up three to four layers.

You will need

- Frame with reverse moulding, with a flat front border approximately 25 mm (1 inch) wide
- Newspaper torn into small squares
- Nylon-reinforced (non-firing) modelling clay

- 2 tablespoons of plain white flour
- Petroleum jelly or cooking oil
- 1 sheet of card
- White emulsion paint
- Green, blue and white acrylic paint
- Gold poster paint

- PVA glue
- Modelling tools
- Piece of board
- Scissors
- Craft knife
- Paint brushes

Card

Modelling tools

Torn newspaper

Paint brush

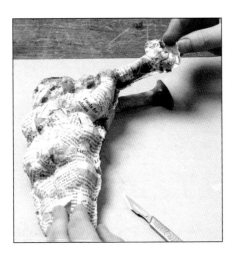

4 When the papier mâché is completely dry, gently prise the papier mâché form off the clay model. You may need to use a sharp knife to loosen the edges.

5 Draw around the base of the clay model onto a piece of card and cut out the shape. Use a craft knife to trim any rough edges from the papier mâché cherub. Fix the base to the underside with overlapping papier mâché squares.

6 When the papier mâché cherub is dry, apply two to three coats of white emulsion, allowing each coat to dry before applying the next. Prime the frame in the same way.

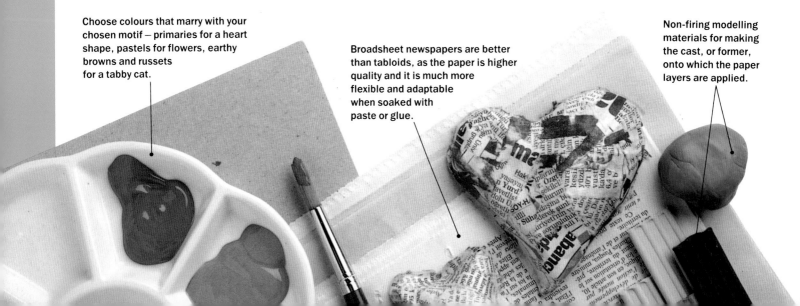

Choose colours that marry with your chosen motif — primaries for a heart shape, pastels for flowers, earthy browns and russets for a tabby cat.

Broadsheet newspapers are better than tabloids, as the paper is higher quality and it is much more flexible and adaptable when soaked with paste or glue.

Non-firing modelling materials for making the cast, or former, onto which the paper layers are applied.

7 Fix the cherub to a corner of the frame with PVA glue. When the glue is dry, paint the frame and cherub in pale turquoise acrylic paint, mixed from blue, green and white. Add extra white to the paint for the cherub for emphasis.

8 When dry, paint both the cherub and frame with gold poster paint. When this is almost dry, carefully wipe away some of the gold with a soft cloth. Repeat if necessary to achieve the effect you want.

Gouache paint is more matt than acrylic paint, and produces sizzling pastel shades. Because it is water-based, wait until the papier mâché is thoroughly dry before decorating.

Finished frame The cherub's eyes are painted with a fine watercolour brush. This finishing touch completes the frame.

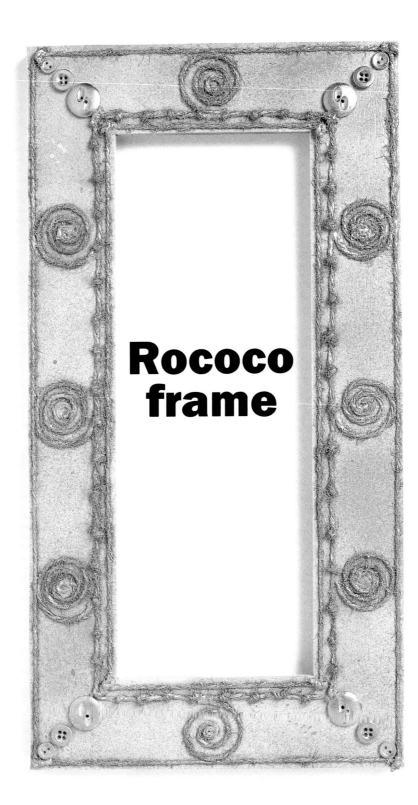

Rococo frame

You will need

- Rectangular frame with flat moulding
- Acrylic primer or undercoat
- PVA glue
- String
- White and gold spray paint
- 12 buttons (4 each of three different sizes)
- Water-based gold size
- Gold powder
- Scissors
- Fine glasspaper
- Small watercolour brush
- Small bristle brush
- Medium paint brush

This rococo-style frame belies its simple – and inexpensive – origins. The string and buttons that give it texture are lifted from their ordinariness by the gold highlighting.

1 Seal the frame with primer/undercoat. Allow to dry and sand lightly. Cut four lengths of string, each at least 100 mm (4 inches) longer than the sides of the frame. Use a fine watercolour brush to apply a line of glue about 6 mm (¼ inch) in from the outside edge of the frame. Press the string in place along each edge, allowing an overlap of 50 mm (2 inches) at each end. Hold in position until firmly stuck. Knot the loose ends at each corner.

2 Cut four lengths of string for the inside edge of the frame and stick down and knot at the corners in the same way. Seal the knots with glue and trim the loose ends.

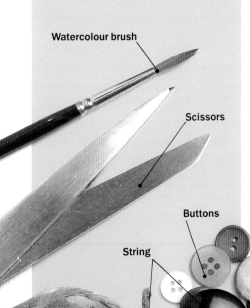

Watercolour brush

Scissors

Buttons

String

Glasspaper

PVA glue

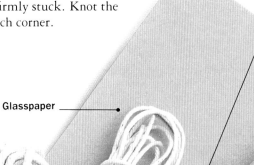

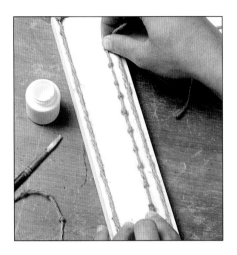

3 Cut four further lengths of string, making each piece twice as long as the inside edge. Make knots at regular intervals along the string, leaving 50 mm (2 inches) at each end unknotted. Apply a line of glue about 12 mm (½ inch) inside the inner string border and stick down the knotted lengths of string, leaving the ends loose, until the glue is dry. Knot at the corners, seal with glue and trim the excess string.

4 Stick a set of three buttons at each corner along the line of the mitre. Place the largest button nearest the inside.

5 Next apply the spiral decorations. For each spiral paint a circle of glue onto the frame and gradually wind the string into place pressing it firmly into the glue. Apply extra glue to the raw edges, to prevent fraying.

Coins can be used instead of buttons for the corners.

Wire can be used instead of string to create a raised effect around the edge of the frame.

Metallic paints for creating a gilded or silvered effect are shown here.

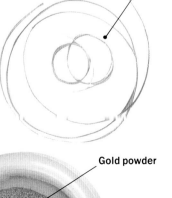

Gold powder

6 Spray the whole frame with white spray paint, following manufacturer's instructions. When dry, spray lightly with gold paint. Apply water-based gold size to the areas to be gilded – buttons and string. Be careful to apply the size only where you wish the gold powder to stick.

7 Use a small brush to dust gold powder sparingly over the sized areas.

Finished frame To remove gold powder that had stuck where it was not wanted, the frame was rubbed carefully with a cloth dampened with white spirit.

Tubes of gold and silver glitter for adding sparkle.

Spray paint

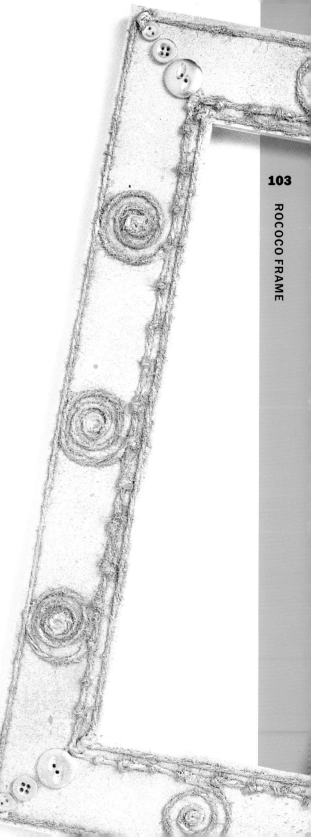

5

More than just paint

*Look no further than your paint
store for the materials to create a
wealth of paint decoration. Applied
with a brush or rag, these traditional
paint and glaze recipes produce a
look that is suitable for any home.
Your choice of colours will ensure
that these classic effects provide the
ideal enhancement to your
photographs, prints and paintings.*

Dragged frame

This frame uses a simple but highly effective traditional method of applying a tinted glaze. By choosing appropriate colours, you can easily adapt this method for a variety of images.

1 Paint the frame with two coats of cream eggshell paint, allowing the paint to dry between coats. When dry, stick masking tape over the corners along one side of the mitre joint.

2 Mix two level tablespoons of glaze with a half tablespoon of white spirit and a small squeeze of blue oil paint. Apply the coloured glaze mixture to two opposite sides of the frame. Use long strokes of the same brush to "drag" the surface evenly.

3 Using a rag, wipe the glaze from some of the mouldings to give more depth. Remove the masking tape from the corners and wipe off any glaze that has overlapped the tape. Keep the unused glaze in a closed jar. Wait 24 hours and then repeat the process on the two remaining sides. There is no need to use masking tape this time. Any glaze that overlaps the previously painted sides can be wiped away with a clean rag. Leave to dry and then varnish.

You will need

- Rectangular frame with curved reverse moulding
- Masking tape
- 25 mm (1 inch) flat paint brush
- Transparent oil glaze
- White spirit
- Blue oil paint
- Cream eggshell paint
- Acrylic varnish
- Rag

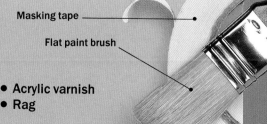

Masking tape

Flat paint brush

Ragged frame

This classic paint-effect frame would provide a distinguished setting for a monochrome print or engraving or a formal photograph. This method depends for its success on the subtlety of the contrast between the toning colours.

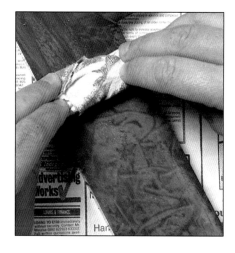

1 Paint the frame with two coats of green eggshell paint. Mix two level tablespoons of glaze with a half tablespoon of white spirit and some dark green enamel paint.

2 Apply the coloured glaze with a brush evenly over the whole frame and sides.

3 While the glaze is still wet, roughly form a clean rag into a sausage shape and roll over the surface and sides of the frame to create a textured effect.

When the frame is dry, apply a coat of varnish. To add a finishing touch, draw a fine line around the edge of the frame with a gold felt-tip pen with the aid of a ruler.

Gold felt-tip pen

Varnish

Enamel paint

Eggshell paint

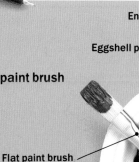

You will need

- **Rectangular frame with wide reverse moulding**
- **Mid green eggshell paint**
- **Dark green enamel paint**
- **Transparent oil glaze**
- **White spirit**
- **12 mm (½ inch) flat paint brush**
- **Cotton rag**
- **Gold felt-tip pen**
- **Varnish**

Flat paint brush

Antiqued frame

This classic finish is not difficult to achieve – it gives an aged impression, perhaps of an antique that has been passed down through the generations. This frame would be perfect for displaying an old etching.

1 Apply two coats of grey emulsion to the entire frame and leave to dry. Mix some white emulsion into the grey and, using a small watercolour brush, pick out areas between the mouldings with this lighter shade.

2 When the paint is dry, mix up an antiquing glaze from two tablespoons of transparent oil glaze to half a tablespoon of white spirit and a small amount of raw umber oil paint. Brush the glaze over the frame, making sure that the paint penetrates the recesses in the mouldings.

3 While the glaze is still wet, lightly wipe over the surface with a rag, applying uneven pressure to make some areas lighter than others.

You will need

- Rectangular frame with a swept moulding
- Grey emulsion
- White emulsion
- 12 mm (½ inch) flat paint brush
- Small watercolour brush
- Transparent oil glaze
- White spirit
- Raw umber oil paint
- Rag

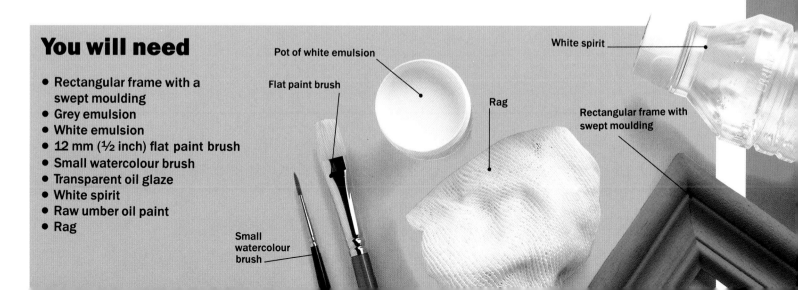

White spirit

Pot of white emulsion

Flat paint brush

Rag

Rectangular frame with swept moulding

Small watercolour brush

Gilded frame

Wonderfully well-suited to a traditional-style oil painting or mirror, this gilded frame also carries oriental associations. It would suit being hung in an opulent room setting.

1 Paint the frame with two coats of red paint. When it is dry, apply a coat of gold size. Wait 15 minutes until the surface is tacky.

2 Pick up the gold leaf with the tracing paper still attached and randomly apply small areas, gold side down, to the frame so that only small pieces stick to it. Allow cracks of red to show between the gold areas to create a crazed effect. Continue until you have covered the frame.

3 Pick up any pieces of gold leaf that fall off and press them back onto the frame – do not worry about overlapping. Use a dry soft brush to brush lightly over the frame to remove any excess gold. If you find the gold too bright, when the frame is dry, you can tone it down by applying a coat of transparent oil glaze mixed with a small amount of burnt umber oil paint.

You will need

- Red emulsion or acrylic paint
- Dutch metal leaf in sheets
- Gold size
- Two 12 mm (½ inch) paint brushes

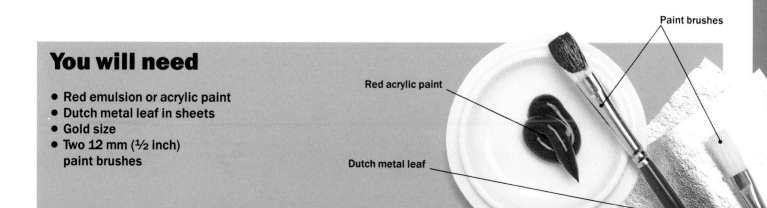

Paint brushes

Red acrylic paint

Dutch metal leaf

Crackle glazed frame

This traditional aged effect is ideal for framing old prints or watercolours. Choose a colour for the banding that complements one of the key colours in the image.

1 Paint the frame with two coats of cream eggshell, allowing the paint to dry between coats. Use a brush to pick out a narrow line of moulding in another colour – in this case red. Allow to dry. Apply the oil-based varnish evenly over the whole frame with a varnish brush, using brush strokes in one direction only. When the oil varnish is just dry enough to be slightly tacky, apply the water-based varnish evenly over the frame using a clean, dry varnish brush.

2 Leave the frame in a warm place – for example, next to a hot water system or inside an airing cupboard. An alternative is to use a hair drier, but it is important to keep the hot air moving over the frame surface to prevent it from scorching. As the varnish dries, cracks will appear. The greater the heat, the more cracks will form. Leave the frame for an hour and then apply some oil-based antiquing glaze. Rub in well so that the whole surface looks dark brown.

3 Before the glaze dries, take a rag and gently rub the whole frame to remove the excess glaze from the surface while leaving the dark brown colour in the cracks. Apply a final coat of oil-based varnish when dry.

Varnish brush

Flat paint brush

Small watercolour brush

You will need

- **Frame with swept moulding**
- **Oil-based varnish**
- **Water-based varnish**
- **Cream eggshell paint**

- **Red eggshell paint**
- **Antiquing oil glaze strongly coloured with raw umber (see page 111, step 2)**

- **12 mm (½ inch) flat paint brush**
- **Small watercolour brush**
- **Varnish brushes**
- **Rag**

Gold spattered frame

You will need

- Rectangular frame with flat moulding.
- Green emulsion or acrylic paint
- Raw umber acrylic paint
- Gold powder
- Methylated spirits
- Emulsion glaze
- Spray varnish
- Two 12 mm (½ inch) paint brushes
- Craft knife with a new blade

Create a verdigris effect with the spattering technique described here. A gold spattered frame can look wonderful surrounding an oil painting or mirror.

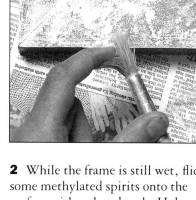

1 Paint the frame with two coats of green paint. Mix four tablespoons of water with a half tablespoon of emulsion glaze. Dip a brush into the glaze mixture and then into a little raw umber paint followed by the gold powder. Working on a horizontal surface, spread the colour roughly all over the frame using extra glaze mixture to make the surface very wet.

2 While the frame is still wet, flick some methylated spirits onto the surface with a clean brush. Holes will develop in the painted surface creating an interesting decorative effect. When the frame is dry, spray with varnish to seal the surface.

Gold powder, available from art materials suppliers.

Paint brushes

Unibond

Frame with flat moulding

Methylated spirits

Stencilled frame

You will need

- Rectangular frame with curved moulding
- Acrylic paint (green, white, blue and yellow)
- Tracing paper
- Acetate
- Scalpel with a new blade
- Round bristle brush
- Cutting mat or thick wad of newspaper
- Pen and ink
- Chinagraph
- Ruler
- Pencil

Stencilling is one of the best-known decorative paint techniques. It can be used to create wonderful repeat designs of flowers, animals or geometric forms.

1 Measure the dimensions of the frame surround so that you can draw the design to the correct dimensions. Work out a repeating design on paper, paying particular attention to how the pattern repeats will work at the corners.

2 Trace the design in ink when you are satisfied with the result.

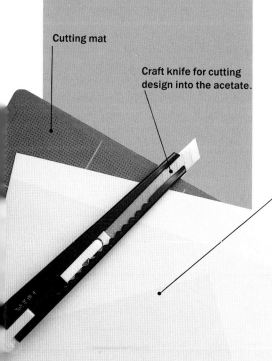

Cutting mat

Craft knife for cutting design into the acetate.

Acetate for making stencil.

Tracing paper

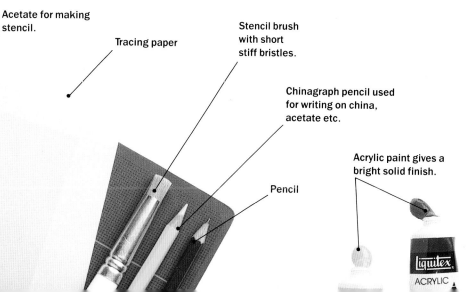

Stencil brush with short stiff bristles.

Chinagraph pencil used for writing on china, acetate etc.

Pencil

Acrylic paint gives a bright solid finish.

Liquitex ACRYLIC

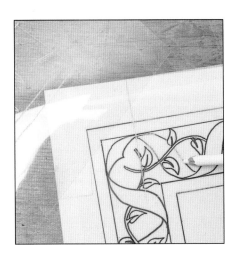

3 Mark a single repeat of the design. Trace each element of the design onto acetate with a chinagraph pencil. Use a separate piece for each element of the design.

4 Using a sharp scalpel and working on a cutting mat or wad of newspaper, carefully cut out the stencil from the acetate.

5 Work out a colour scheme, choosing a different colour for each element of the design. Paint the frame in your chosen background colour – in this case green. Allow the paint to dry thoroughly.

When designing stencils or templates, choose simple shapes. Designs can be drawn freehand or traced from books or magazines, if you're not confident of your drawing skills.

Templates cut from card. Paint or draw around the outside to transfer the design to your chosen frame.

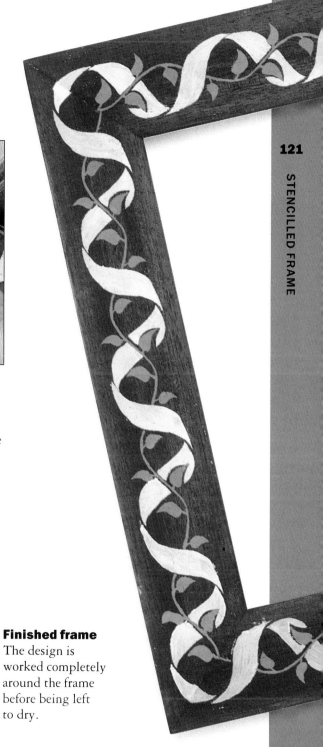

6 Start with the element of design that is to be in the lightest colour – in this case the "ribbon" motif. Lay the stencil in its planned position in one corner of the frame. Holding it firmly in place, brush the paint over the stencil. The paint should be mixed to a thick consistency. Avoid brushing the paint under the stencil by using circular brush movements. Carefully peel up the stencil and replace it in the next position required.

7 When you have completed all the repeats of the first stencil, allow the paint to dry before applying the next element of the design. This should be in a darker colour. Position the new stencil over the appropriate area of the design and apply paint as before.

Stiff card can be used instead of acetate, though it isn't so effective because the edges go soggy after continued use. Coated card is best as it repels paint and can be wiped clean after use.

Finished frame
The design is worked completely around the frame before being left to dry.

Terms and techniques

The following is a glossary of possibly unfamiliar terms and includes instructions for several basic techniques.

Glossary of terms

If you're starting out crafting you won't be familiar with all the terms used in this book. Below, definitions are supplied.

Acrylic paint This is a common type of artist's paint that is widely available from art materials suppliers. It is water soluble while wet and water resistant when dry. Used "straight from the tube", it produces solid, matt colour, but it can be diluted for use as a thin wash.

Acetate Stiff, clear film available in pads from art supply shops.

Artist's oil paints A range of high-quality colours. Used for tinting oil-based paints, glazes (see *transparent oil glaze*) or *varnish*.

Bradawl A woodworking tool with a metal point that is used for making starting holes for screws and nails.

Casein-based paint A type of water-based paint that dries to a water-resistant finish. It is especially suitable for projects where a strong, flat colour is desired.

Craft knife This is an essential item for tasks that require accurate cutting of paper or card. It consists of a handle fitted with a sturdy, but sharp blade that can be removed and replaced if it becomes blunt. Various types are available from hardware stores and craft suppliers.

Dutch metal leaf A type of imitation gold leaf. It is cheaper and easier to handle than genuine gold leaf. It is sold in sheets that can then be cut to size.

Eggshell paint This is an oil-based paint with a slight sheen, useful as a base for oil glazes (see *transparent oil glaze*), and available in a range of colours.

Emulsion glaze This product is available from specialist paint suppliers. It is used in home-decorating to make wallpaper – for example, in bathrooms – resistant to water. In frame-decorating it is used to create paint effects.

Escutcheon pins Fine brass pins which don't split wood when hammered in.

Gilt cream This is a gold-coloured wax that is useful for restoring old gilt frames. It can be rubbed onto a frame with a cloth or finger and then buffed to a lustrous finish. It can be bought from art materials suppliers.

"Gold" powder Metallic powders are actually made from finely powdered bronze. They are available from art materials suppliers in different shades of gold and silver. Such powders can be mixed with a medium such as shellac or applied over gold size to achieve a gilded finish on a frame.

Gold size A sticky solution that is used to fix gold or imitation gold leaf to a surface. There are two types available: oil- and water-based. The former provides stronger adhesion, but dries quickly and is therefore more difficult to work with. Water-based gold size dries more slowly and is probably the best choice for the novice gilder. Available from art and craft suppliers.

Impact adhesive A type of glue, widely available from DIY stores, that provides a strong and immediate bond. It should be applied to both surfaces and left for 10 minutes before joining the parts.

Mitre The 45-degree angle cut made in each end of a piece of frame *moulding* so that they meet at a 90-degree angle (mitre joint).

Modelling clay (non-firing) Self-hardening modelling clay.

Modelling tools Special hand-held tools with different ends (flat, pointed, etc) used for shaping clay and to create different surface effects.

Moulding A shaped length of wood used to make picture frames (see opposite page).

Primer The term used to describe any substance that is applied to a surface to prepare it for painting. Most hardware stores sell proprietary primers for use on bare wood. These can be used before applying paint to your frame.

PVA glue A multi-purpose, quick-drying glue that can be used on paper, metal, wood, etc. It can also be thinned with water for use in pastes for making papier mâché (see page 125) and as a *sealant*.

Quilling paper Long strips of 3mm (⅛ inch) wide paper. Available from craft supply shops in packs of assorted and separate colours. (See page 126.)

Quilling tool Plastic or metal implement used for making paper coils. The tool has a slot at one end, into which the end of the *quilling paper* strips are slipped. (See page 126.)

Sealant A solution that is painted onto a surface to prevent it "bleeding" or otherwise affecting painted or other decorative treatments applied over it. Several different types of sealant may be used, such as *shellac* and thinned *PVA glue* as well as proprietary sanding sealants and knotting solutions.

Shellac A traditional alcohol-based lacquer that is used as a *sealant*.

Transparent oil glaze An oil-based medium which can be tinted. Its exceptional covering power makes it relatively cheap, and it dries slowly,

giving time for it to be worked on.

Varnish (flat finish/satin finish/spray finish/oil-based/water-based) Hard-wearing finish designed to protect surfaces, and available in matt, satin (semi-matt) or gloss. Can be applied by brush or spray, and is available as oil-based or water-based; the former is quicker drying (a couple of hours) but requires at least two coats to create a good finish; the latter takes longer to dry (about seven hours) but needs only one coat. Always apply varnish to a clean, dry surface. Use a good quality flat brush reserved for this purpose.

Whiting This white powder is used as a thickening agent in gilding work and papier mâché. Available from artist's suppliers.

Wood stain A liquid that alters the colour of wood without leaving a surface film or obscuring the grain, available from hardware stores.

Preparing the frame

When buying a ready-made raw wood frame, choose one that is smooth and free of knots and other imperfections. If there are cracks in the frame –

usually at the corners – fill these with a proprietary wood filler, leave to dry then sand down.

For second-hand frames from junk shops or boot sales, sand down the surface enough to obtain a key to which the paint can adhere. Check for cracks and use wood filler if necessary.

Frame mouldings

These can be bought in a huge variety of shapes and sizes. You can either buy them ready-made or make them yourself, if you know how. Most of the frames in this book require only simple shapes.

1 Basic flat moulding Can be narrow or wide. Most of the decorative techniques in this book require a wide moulding.

2 Reverse moulding Raised at the inner edge. May be flat or curved.

3 Swept moulding Raised at the outer edge. May be flat or curved.

4 Cassetta-style moulding Has a flat surround between raised inner and outer borders.

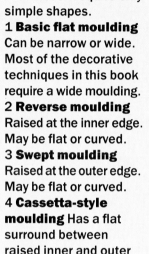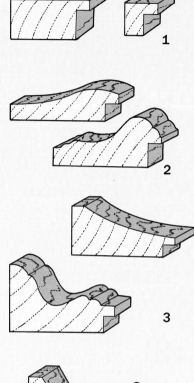

Mounts

Many images benefit from being displayed in a mount. This can serve several purposes. First it keeps the image from being in direct, prolonged contact with the glass. This is essential for any image on paper such as a watercolour or drawing

Parts of a frame

Frames have several parts:
1 **Frame**.
2 **Glass**, usually 2 mm thick, and cut to the correct measure.
3 **Mount** Specially made piece of card, into which a window is cut with square or bevelled edges.
4 **Picture**, attached to the back of the mount.
5 **Backing board** Made from masonite, plywood or thick card.

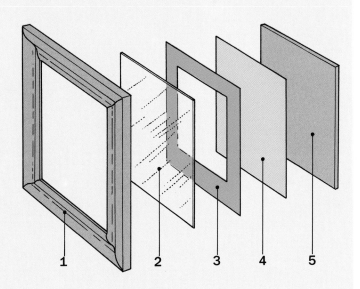

1   2   3   4   5

that may be damaged as a result of such contact. In addition, adding a border allows you to use a larger frame, thereby making a bolder feature of the image. Moreover, a carefully considered mount can considerably add to the visual impact of the frame and image.

Types of mount The simplest mounts are made of special mountboard with a bevel-edge window for the image. These can be made relatively easily yourself if you have a mount cutter for cutting the bevelled edges. However, you can also buy ready-made mounts or have one made by a commercial picture-framer to the size you need. Always choose acid-free or acid-neutral mountboard for any image of lasting value. Cheaper boards may damage the paper of your image over a long period.

Choosing a mount The mount you choose must work well with both the image and the frame. It is traditional to choose a colour that subtlely echoes the colours in the picture. Another approach is to pick a colour that contrasts strongly with the image, thereby "setting it off" effectively. This also helps to provide a visual "distance" between the image and frame.

You can make more elaborate mounts by adding painted or collaged decoration in suitable colours. Fine lines painted around the window can give added emphasis. You may consider covering the mount with fabric, or decorated paper, or it can be given a textured finish by painting it with a layer of gesso. (Use extra thick board for this last method.) A double-mount, in which a second mount with a slightly larger window is placed over the first mount, can also be effective.

Size of mount There are no hard and fast rules for deciding the size of the mount. But it is important that it should not be too narrow or the picture will look cramped in the frame. Conversely, if the mount is too wide, the image may be "lost". The usual rule is to have the top and side borders of the mount of equal width and the lower border slightly deeper.

Frame fixings

Most ready-made frames come with their own fixings so that all you will need to do to hang the picture is to attach a length of picture wire or cord. If, however, your frame is without fixings then you will need to attach your own.

1 **Screw eyes** Screw these into the back of the frame, approximately one quarter of the height of the frame down from the top. This will ensure that the frame hangs at the correct angle from the wall. Attach a length of picture cord or wire and suspend from a picture pin so that the cord is hidden behind the frame.

2 **Picture pins** These can be bought from most hardware stores. A fine pin, inserted through a brass hook, is hammered into the wall at a downwards angle. This

Recipes

PAPIER MACHE PULP

This is used for creating relief designs on the frame surround. It consists of torn paper, usually newsprint, soaked in water and glue to produce a pulp that can be moulded and shaped. Papier mâché pulp can be painted or gilded when dry. Many craftworkers develop their own recipes. Two alternatives are given here.

Method 1

- 2 double-page sheets of broadsheet newspaper
- 1 tablespoon whiting
- 1 tablespoon PVA glue
- ½ tablespoon linseed oil
- 1 tablespoon wallpaper paste powder

Tear newspaper into 25 mm (1 inch) squares, place in a saucepan and cover with water. Leave to soak overnight. Add approximately 1 litre of water. Boil the mixture for half an hour to loosen fibres. Allow to cool a little. Put the soaked paper in a blender while still warm. Reduce it to a pulp. You can use a hand whisk if you don't have a blender. Strain off as much water as possible and compress the pulp in your hand to squeeze out excess water. Do not compress too much or it will form a solid ball. Put the pulp in a bucket or bowl and stir in all the other ingredients.

Method 2

- Approximately 10 sheets of newspaper
- 3 tablespoons of interior filler
- 2 tablespoons of PVA glue

Tear the newspaper into small pieces and place in a bucket. Add enough boiling water to cover and leave to soak for about 2 hours. Use an electric hand blender to chop the soaked paper to a pulp, adding water as necessary. Strain through a sieve and mix with the filler and glue.

GESSO

This is a thin paste applied to a surface to create a smooth ground on which to paint. It may be applied over papier mâché relief work.

- ⅓ cup of PVA wood glue
- ⅓ cup of water
- ⅓ cup of whiting

Dilute PVA glue with an equal amount of water and stir thoroughly. Sift in the whiting gradually, stirring constantly to make a cream consistency.

TINTED GLAZES

Colour-tinted transparent glazes are used to create a number of decorative paint effects. You can buy the colourless glaze base, sometimes known as scumble, from specialist paint suppliers. Tint this, if required, with artist's oil paint thinned with a little white spirit. Add this a little at a time until you achieve the strength of colour you want. Always mix more tinted glaze than you think you will need; it may be difficult to match the colour precisely if you need to make a second batch.

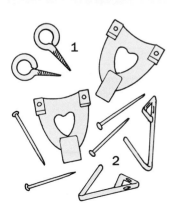

holds the hook securely in place, but can be removed, leaving only a small hole in the wall. Larger hooks with two fixing pins are available, and should be used for heavy frames.

Cord and chain Both are suitable for most frames. If you choose cord, make sure that it is nylon, which is stronger and lasts longer than ordinary string. Chain is used for large, heavy frames.

Hanging your pictures

The effect of a stunning combination of frame and picture can easily be diminished if they are hung without due thought. While many terrific effects are obtained by breaking the rules, here are some basic guidelines to help you.

Wall colour Consider the colours of the frame and picture in relation to the walls of the room. Many of the framing ideas in this book use bright colours. These may look best on a plain white or neutral coloured wall. However, a wall colour that echoes a colour used in the frame may also work well. Frames of muted colours or metallics can be lost on a wall that is too close in tone. Try to ensure adequate contrast between frame and wall. A multicolour frame may not work well with a patterned wallpaper, especially if the pattern is large. A plainer frame may be better in this situation.

Position Pictures should ideally be hung at an average eye level. This may not, however, always be possible – for example, when hanging pictures in a vertical group. Large pictures are best in a position in which people can stand back to get a good view. Smaller pictures are ideal for more confined spaces where they can benefit from close attention. Always try to avoid placing pictures too close to radiators or other direct sources of heat. They should also be protected from moisture.

Groups and arrangements A simple rule is that while a large frame will look good on a wall on its own, smaller frames often benefit from grouping. However, the highly decorated frames in this book may require a little bending of this rule. It is possible that the visual impact of these frames could be reduced if placed with other decorated frames. A small decorated frame may be shown to its best advantage on its own in a narrow space – for example, between two windows.

If you decide to hang your frames in a group, experiment with the arrangement by laying the pictures out on the floor.

Quilling

Quilling is a technique in which rolled paper strips are glued to a surface in a variety of patterns. This can be used to great effect for decorating frames.

Books of quilling paper in assorted colours can be bought from craft suppliers. You can roll the paper by hand, but most people find it easier to use a quilling tool. Glue the finished quilled decoration to the frame surface by applying PVA glue to the back of each piece. Instructions for creating some basic quilled patterns are given below.

1 Coils Coil a length of quilling paper tightly around the tool and glue the end of the main body of the coil. The length of your paper strip will determine the diameter of the circle. For a looser effect, release the coil and allow it to expand slightly before gluing.

2 Cone Make a tight coil and gently push out the centre with a pointed tool such as a cocktail stick.

3 Teardrop Make a loose coil as above and pinch one side.

4 Lozenge Make a loose coil and pinch opposite sides.

5 Square Make a lozenge and then turn and pinch the opposite sides.

6 Heart Make a loose coil. Press in one side and gently pinch on either side of the indentation and pinch the side opposite.

7 Scroll Roll part of the paper strip into a loose coil, leaving the end unrolled.

8 Bunny ears Make a coil, and indent the top.

9, 10, 11, 12 Double scrolls Scroll one end of the strip as above and then roll the loose end in the opposite direction to form an S scroll (9). Roll the loose end in the same direction as the first to form a C scroll (10). Make a V scroll (11) by pinching the centre of a C scroll from the inside. An open heart scroll (12) is formed by pinching the outside of a C scroll.

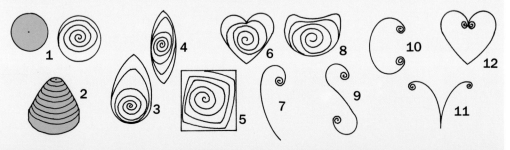

Index

Credits

With special thanks to Jane Quigley of the London Picture Frame Co Ltd, 70 New Kings Road, London SW6 4LT, who supplied the wooden frames.

With many thanks to all the talented craftspeople who designed and made the frames:

Madeleine Adams Driftwood frame; Beachcomber frame
Clare Baggaley Lobster frame
Janet Cooper and **Marion Wright** Quilled paper; Pressed flowers frame
Graham Day Multi-image frame; Marbled paper frame; Music lovers frame; Postcard frame
Gill Dickinson Wire and bead frame; Woodland frame; Wound string frame; String frame
Sarah Doe Dragged frame; Gilded frame; Ragged frame; Gold spattering; Crackle glaze; Antiqued
Vivien Frank Patchwork frame; Ribbon-weave frame; Toy frame
Sandra Hurst Chico China mosaic; Sunflowers frame; Cherub frame; Stencilled and painted
Sally Richmond Seeds frame; Oriental eggshell frame; Gesso and gilded; Rococo frame
Natalie Rule Glittering sweet-wrap frame; Cartoon-character frame; Victorian découpage; Holiday memento frame

All other frames were designed and made by the author.